CHICAGO'S SERIAL HUSBAND

CHICAGO'S SERIAL HUSBAND

The Marriages & Murders of Johann Hoch

ADAM SELZER

Published by The History Press
An imprint of Arcadia Publishing
Charleston, SC
www.historypress.com

First published 2025

Manufactured in the United States

ISBN 9781467158589
Hardcover ISBN 9781540299987

Library of Congress Control Number: 2025941129

CONTENTS

A Note on Names 7
Introduction: February 1905, Nickel Plate Railroad 11

1. Wheeling, 1895 15
2. The Wives and Crimes of Johann Hoch 21
3. Marie, Emilie, and Bertha: The Schippnick Sisters 47
4. Circulation Wars 55
5. The Story Unfolds 61
6. Evelyn Campbell's Quest 65
7. Like Zithers for Him 71
8. Captured 78
9. Nights on Mulberry Street 83
10. The Wives at the Inquest 88
11. Anna Hendricks in New York 90
12. The Ordeal of the Black Pen 97
13. The Road to Chicago 101
14. Back in Town 108
15. The Inquest Continues 113

16. The Ladies Can't Resist You When You Look Like Johann Hoch 118
17. Tales from the Murder Castle 122
18. The Old Jail 126
19. On Trial 132
20. A New Reporter Enters the Saga 139
21. To Beat the Gallows 143
22. Justice for the Poor 147
23. The Pardon Board 155
24. The Final Day 161
25. Through with the World 165
26. The Aftermath 173

Epilogue 179
Appendix: Known Wives 189
Notes 193
About the Author 208

A NOTE ON NAMES

Historically, babies in Germany were given a first name (often Johann for boys, Mary or Anna for girls) and a *rufname* (middle name), which they would usually go by. Johann Sebastian Bach, for instance, would have gone by Sebastian; his five brothers all had "Johann" for a first name.

In the late nineteenth and early twentieth centuries, when Johann Hoch was on his American crime spree, German immigrants in the United States often alternated freely between not only their two names but also between their German (Johann) and Anglicized forms (John).

Additionally, nearly every woman connected to Hoch not only alternated between their two names, with multiple spellings and variations, but also had several surnames over the course of their lives. His first American wife was variously called Karoline Miller, Catherine Hoch, Karolina Hoh, Karoline Huff and Caroline Huff.

A great many of his wives commonly went by Mary or Maria, and this has led to much confusion; from the start, people who compiled lists of Hoch's victims were often unaware that "Mary Hoch" and "Julia Steinbrecher" were the same person.

I've attempted to use one name consistently for each person, sometimes favoring a name they may have used less frequently themselves, just to differentiate between them. For last names, I've generally used the spelling that appears on their tombstones, when one could be found.

The *New York American* portrays Hoch aboard a train to Chicago. Reporters Frances Maule and Evelyn Campbell can be seen on the right. *From the* New York American.

INTRODUCTION

FEBRUARY 1905, NICKEL PLATE RAILROAD

The train from New York crept alongside snowdrifts and barren farmland, slowly lurching toward the Windy City. February 1905 was a cold month; papers in Chicago were offering tips on what to wear and what to eat to manage in the freezing weather ("lots of fat"). Snowstorms had slowed the train considerably, but the mood aboard was light, almost like a party.

Someone asked Johann Hoch, the most famous passenger aboard, to come have a drink.

"No sir," said Hoch. "I go nowhere except where Sergeant Detective Loftus goes."

Hoch was handcuffed to Loftus, so he didn't have much of a choice. The train was carrying him to Chicago, where he was facing several charges of bigamy and at least one charge of murder. Authorities there had already announced that they intended to hang him. But he seemed unconcerned. He was making jokes out of everything.

When a newsboy came through selling magazines, Hoch asked for the latest thing he had on architecture.

"Are you an architect, Mr. Hoch?" someone asked.

"No, I ain't an architect. The newspapers say I am a butcher!"

"Well, *are* you a butcher?"

"No, I couldn't kill a cat. I'm what you call a mechanic."[1]

Some reporters transcribed his dialogue phonetically, in his broad German accent. ("How many of dose vimmin vill be at der depot?") Many likened him to a German dialect comedian.

"What are the white powders said by the police to be poisons?" one reporter asked.

"Ach, those powders they found in my pen, I used to wash my teeth to make my teeth white. The powders in Chicago are headache powders."[2]

The *New York Telegram* had just run an article about Hoch in which a subheading read, "Not an Attractive Man."[3] "He is short and fat," they wrote. "His forehead retreats and his chin bulges." The *Chicago Journal* would say Hoch was "about as far from being handsome as mud is from being ice cream," with "a high forehead like a cow's" and a nose "more resembling a chunk of putty."[4]

But some believed that this unattractive man had married over fifty women.

And murdered several of them.

"In a low comedy way," wrote Frances Maule, a New York reporter who met him on the train, "he is what is popularly known as 'good company,' an amusing, mildly cynical sort of fellow, with a vital and virile flow of spirits. One could imagine such a man bringing into the dull, drab existence of the ordinary, rent-haunted hausfrau of the German districts in Chicago a glimpse of the brighter and merrier life." She knew exactly the type of women he targeted from her own Chicago days.

The year 1905 was an incredible time for journalism; technology was changing the way news was gathered, reported and presented. Publishing photographs had only recently become affordable and effective, and papers like Hearst's *Chicago American* were using them like a kid with a new toy. The competition among papers was fierce and often literally violent, but among reporters, there was a sense of camaraderie. Reporting would become a *profession* soon—the first journalism schools would open in a few years—but for now, it was still a job they were all making up as they went along.

And Hoch had been helping them sell papers. The rush to piece together his life story—and to find and arrest him—had been dominating the front pages of many papers for three weeks now. Ambrose Bierce had written a poem about him. Popular columnist Helen Rowland had weighed in. Evelyn Campbell, a reporter who'd become a "special commissioner" for the police on the case, sat across from him for most of the train ride. She'd turned detective in her *Chicago American* column, uncovering tales of Hoch's life before journeying to New York to interview him in person. On the train, he gave her great quotes in between antagonizing and insulting her.

At every station, crowds waited to see the prisoner, the sensation of the year. At some stops, Hoch would shout, "You are all loafers!" At others, he'd blow kisses.

When things were quiet, he provided Detective Loftus will funny epigrams, such as, "When a man marries, he swears to love. After he's married, he loves to swear!"

"The smilingest little dutchman who ever poisoned a wife," Loftus whispered to a reporter.[5]

It had barely been two months since Johann Hoch had married Marie Schippnick Walcker in Chicago. On January 12, five weeks after the wedding, she had died of an apparent kidney disease. While her body was still on the bed, Hoch proposed to her sister, Emilie Fischer. Emilie accepted the day after the funeral, and the two were married on January 18. Within twenty-four hours, he'd gotten her to take her money out of the bank and vanished with it.

After a highly publicized manhunt, he was captured in New York and held there until the paperwork to bring him back to Illinois came through.

Now, Marie's body had been exhumed, and a whole crowd of deserted wives was said to be waiting to greet Hoch at the LaSalle Street Station in Chicago.

Lots of people were waiting there, in fact. Quite a cast of characters were brought together by the Hoch case.

Coroner Peter Hoffman had just taken office weeks before, but he had a long career ahead of him, one that would be mired by allegations of corruption on such a grand scale that while serving as sheriff in the 1920s, he'd end up doing time in his own jail.

Inspector George Shippy had already connected Hoch to all sorts of unsolved cases. Some of his theories about Hoch were so outrageous that they may have been early signs of the dementia that would overtake him within a few years.

Chief O'Neill, best remembered for knocking off police work to study Irish folk songs, was confidently telling reporters that Hoch had killed a dozen women.

Several Chicago women who'd married Hoch were speaking with the police, and many others from around the country were planning to come identify him as the man who'd deserted them, if they could.

Myron Chappell, accused of buying dead bodies from arch-murderer H.H. Holmes to make into articulated skeletons for medical schools in the

1890s, was eager to visit the police station to confirm that Hoch had been a regular in the "Holmes Castle."

And at the center of it all was the great enigma himself, Johann Hoch. He looked, to twenty-first-century eyes, like the guy on the Pringles can. He talked like a German character on *The Simpsons*. But he had a particular skill with women: he could find out what they wanted and be that guy for a month.

Every day, more women were coming forward claiming to have married him.

Who were all of these women? Which did he really marry, and which were mistaking him for someone else? Which of them did he kill? Why had he chosen to kill some of them instead of deserting them? What became of those who survived?

The story of Hoch would be retold several times over the decades, mostly in short articles and chapters in anthologies. But even in 1905, no one could gather all of the details of the story together, and retellings have always been hopeless jumbles of fact, fiction and misinformation. Many of the real answers to these questions would soon be buried in old paperwork and microfilm reels.

Some answers could still be uncovered a century or so later. But others, surely, are still buried with Johann Jacob Schmitt, alias Johann Hoch (among other monikers), in his unmarked grave in the suburbs of Chicago.

1

WHEELING, 1895

Legend has it that in the summer of 1818, when a cargo of ice was delivered to New Orleans, Mayor Macarty had it destroyed immediately, lest he find himself with a public health crisis on his hands. Ice wasn't unknown in the city; there was often some of it on the river in the winter months. But in the summer, people might be tempted to beat the bayou heat by adding it to drinks. And that, the mayor believed, could kill them.

It was a common belief at the time. Dr. Benjamin Rush wrote in 1789 that some summers, four or five people per day would drop dead in Philadelphia alone from drinking ice water.

In 1892, Adolph Hoch, a "well-known and popular" Wheeling, West Virginia mill worker, woke up screaming in pain. Two hours later, he was dead. He'd barely had time to dictate a will and sign it with an "X." The official cause of death for Adolph, who was in his early thirties, was "heart failure," but the local paper blamed "excessively cold ice water" he'd been drinking at the mill. His employer was taken to task for not letting the men cool off with safe, healthy beer.[6]

Adolph and his wife, Caroline Miller Hoch, lived in a largely German neighborhood around Bogg's Run, near the banks of the Ohio River. They had saved enough for Caroline to live comfortably in widowhood, at least for a while, and when the cash ran out, there would be property to sell. By the end of 1894, Caroline hadn't made any known moves to find a new husband.

"ARSENIC ENOUGH IN HER BODY TO CAUSE DEATH"

—*DR. LEWKE on the Mrs. Hock post mortem.*

Coroner's Physician Makes First Complete Statement of the Examination for the Chicago American.

The first full statement of the objective post-mortem examination, anatomical and microscopical, of the body of Mrs. Marie Welker-Hock is herewith presented by the Chicago American. The preliminary report of Dr. Lewke to Coroner Hoffman yesterday was verbal and brief, and the first complete statement of the examination was given to the American last night by Dr. Lewke. The statement shows that a relatively large amount of arsenic was found in the stomach of Mrs. Hock; that the arsenic was in her organs before she was embalmed, and that there was sufficient of the poison to have caused her death.

The detailed report follows:

BY DR. O. W. LEWKE,

Coroner's Physician.

I have found enough arsenic in the stomach of Marie Welker-Hock to have caused death. I found no trace of arsenic in the embalming fluid or in or about the instruments used by the embalmer to preserve her remains.

I found the exhumed body of Mrs. Hock in a good state of preservation, despite the fact that she had been buried for thirteen days, and I was therefore able to make a satisfactory post-mortem examination.

I found an edema of the brain and the blood vessels of the brain and membranes markedly injected. The lungs were edemitous and hardened, the latter due to the embalming fluid. The lungs were slightly adherent to the pleura (the lining membrane.)

The peritoneum was negative; the inside of the heart was hypertrophied (enlarged.) The mitral valve of the heart was hardened and thickened.

The walls of the stomach were thickened, the mucus lining of the stomach thickened and inflamed and containing some dark colored substance.

The peritoneum was negative; the intestines were collapsed and had been punctured in many places by the embalmer. There was a brown atrophy and passive hyperemia of the liver, and an atrophy of **of the stomach showed a relatively large quantity of arsenic.**

I procured samples of the embalming fluid which was used and of another fluid which the undertaker had, but which he assured me he had not used on Mrs. Hock. I also secured the rubber tubing, pump and trocar which he employed in embalming. A thorough analysis of both fluids showed that they contained no arsenic. The instruments I boiled in chemicals which would dissolve any arsenic, and again found no arsenic.

I must therefore conclude that the arsenic was not introduced by the embalmer during the embalming process, and was present in the body prior to Mrs. Hock's death.

Arsenic is a white, tasteless powder, soluble in water and classified as an irritant poison. The action of arsenic varies with the amount administered and the time of administration and the individual susceptibility.

The first symptoms of arsenical poisoning are: Burning in the throat, pain in the pit of the stomach, nausea, vomiting and purging. These are followed in fatal doses by coma and death in from 1 to 5 hours. These symptoms are not always present in all cases.

When a slight dose is administered, for instance, a single grain, there may be pain in the stomach and nausea, followed by vomiting and recovery in twen-

PHOTO WHICH PROVES HOCK MARRIED WOMAN IN WHEELING, W. VA.

This photo is said by the police to show that Hock, then under the name of "Jacob Huff," contracted a marriage with Mrs. Caroline Miller

A newspaper mockup of "Jacob Huff's" wedding photo with Caroline Hoch. *From the* Chicago American.

Justice Arkle, who'd written out Adolph's will, noted that "[Caroline] was blind in one eye, and was an unattractive woman."[7] A city official, Paul Riedel, agreed: "She…was not at all good looking although considered a good, respectable woman."[8]

But early in 1895, a man named Jacob Huff came to town from Germany and purchased a saloon on Jacob Street, a busy thoroughfare that ran along the river. He made an immediate impression in Bogg's Run.

"He was one of the handsomest men I ever saw," Justice Arkle would recall. "A man who would impress anybody, or what you might term 'fascinating.'"[9]

This was a term that would come up to describe this man again and again over the next decade: *fascinating*.

Particularly fascinating was Huff's story that he was one of the survivors of the *Elbe*, a steamship that had collided with another ship in the North Sea just weeks before. Nearly all of the passengers and crew had died before the ship even sank, all of twenty minutes after the collision.[10] Huff's new neighbors and patrons must have hung on every fascinating word as he told of his miraculous survival.

His saloon became the place to be. Huff was not only a spellbinding storyteller, but he was also an easy mark for letting people have their drinks "on tick."[11] He was so free with credit, in fact, that some suspected that the saloon was just "a bluff," covering up some sort of "big game." He almost surely hinted that it was.

Reverend Herman Haass, a minister at St. Matthew's German Lutheran Church, noted that, "For a time [Huff] was a popular fellow. He was something of a musician, playing the zither very well and being able to sing, and at once became an active member of a number of German singing societies in the city."

But Haass sensed that something was off about the stranger who had come to town. "From the time I saw the man I did not like him. I did not like his eyes."

Though Haass didn't know it (and never seems to have figured it out), Huff was absolutely lying about being on the *Elbe.* He had crossed the ocean on the *Stuttgart*, a steamer that reached New York from Bremen more than a week before the *Elbe* went down. His purchase of the saloon had been announced in the local papers on February 3,[12] just a few days after the shipwreck, and long before any *Elbe* survivors could have possibly made it across the ocean.

However, neither of the major Wheeling newspapers had carried a list of the survivors, so even if people still had papers from January in their homes at the end of February, it would have been difficult to check up on Huff's claims. It was hard to look into anything in those days. News was traveling faster than ever before, but it disappeared quickly.

Huff began looking around for a wife and apparently proposed unsuccessfully to a couple of women before he met Caroline Hoch. It seemed an odd match to some in the town. "He was a fine looking man, and everyone who looked at him was surprised at him marrying [Adolph] Hoch's widow," recalled Justice Arkle. "But it was her money that Huff as after."

Despite any misgivings he had about Mr. Huff, Reverend Haass performed the wedding in April 1895. The next month, Huff moved his saloon to suburban Benwood. On June 14, he summoned Haass to his home, where Caroline had taken ill.

"I found her in terrible suffering," Haass told reporters a decade later. "[Huff] had been constantly at her bedside during her illness....I noticed that when he went to the mantel to get a dose of medicine for her a great expression of fear came on her face. He walked over to her, though, kissed her, and then she willingly took the medicine."[13]

Suspecting that Caroline was being poisoned, Haass brought in Dr. Gregory Ackerman, who examined both the patient and the medicines, then simply said, "I will have nothing to do with the case."

Caroline's regular doctor, H.F. Ford, had suspicions as well and had even called in one Dr. William Pipes to consult him on the matter. Pipes advised him to say nothing, "as [we] might get into trouble."[14]

One morning, Haass heard that Mrs. Huff had died. He made his way to the house, where her lifeless body was lying alone and unattended. He found Mr. Huff being shaved at a nearby barbershop.

"When he saw me he dropped his head and seemingly wept bitterly," Haass recalled. "To me, however, there was no indication of affection, and I came to bitterly hate the man at that time....I went back with him to the house, and he kissed his dead wife time and time again....His grief, it seemed to me, was all a mockery."

Caroline was buried near her first husband in Red Men's Cemetery the afternoon after her death. The cause of death was given in records at "gastritis."

Reverend Haass remained vigilant. He began visiting drugstores, asking questions and trying to find out just what sort of drugs Huff had been buying to treat his wife.

Huff, meanwhile, had persuaded Caroline to fill out a will making him her beneficiary before her death, and with the will in his hand, he was able to draw around $1,000 from her various bank accounts. He told neighbors of his plans to build a two-story beer garden and concert hall.

One night, Haass was having dinner when he heard a noise coming from his bedroom. Walking upstairs, he expected to find a burglar, but instead found Jacob Huff.

"I'm sorry," said Huff. "I came to look for you."

With that, Huff backed out of the room. Haass threw out anything in the bedroom that could have been poisoned.

The next morning, a suit of Huff's clothes, with a watch and Caroline's will in the pocket, was found on the banks of the Ohio River. It appeared as though he'd stripped himself naked and then drowned himself.

While police dragged the river for a body, a rumor spread that Caroline's grave appeared to have been disturbed, and people began to wonder out loud if Caroline had been murdered. No formal investigation was made, but few believed that Huff had died. The headline in the *Wheeling Register* summed it up succinctly: "It Deceived Nobody."

For a few days, there were rumors of "Huff" being spotted around southern Ohio and stories that he'd bought a ticket for Chicago right before the phony suicide. But time passed, and the stories died down. Perhaps Caroline's will was suspicious, but so was Adolph's. It was full of language about "my dear wife" that Adolph surely hadn't dictated while he was in the middle of his death throes.

But one telltale clue remained: the inscription inside the watch found among Huff's clothes had been scratched off, but if it was held at the right angle, it could still be read: "Jac. Schmitt."

Haass never stopped believing that "Huff" had been on the *Elbe*, but he knew that he had been inconsistent when telling stories of his past. Once, Huff had said he had worked for a wine merchant in Hoexter, Germany. Other times, he said he was from Bingen-on-the-Rhine.

The early photo that was eventually given to Chicago police by Reverend Haass. *From the* Chicago American.

Inquiries to both towns led to a letter from police, who identified the photo Haass sent as that of Jacob Schmitt, from the tiny town of Horrweiler, some thirty miles from the similarly tiny Bingen. According to the letter, Schmitt was born in 1862 to Adam Schmitt and Elizabeth Weber Schmitt and was married to one Christine Phillipine (or Caroline) Ramb. They had four children, three of whom were still living, but Schmitt had deserted them in January 1895, escaping trouble for financial crimes.[15]

Records to verify all of this are elusive, but German newspapers would fill in more details as "Schmitt" became famous. Young Jacob was said to be intelligent, but given to mischief in school. After being expelled for some forgotten offense, he was an apprentice to his father, a metal worker, and then left home over an argument about a woman. He'd done a stint in the military, opened a tinsmith shop, and worked as a wine dealer. He was recalled as a "proud and high-spirited" person who "tried to 'play the big man' in every situation."[16]

But he became known for crooked deals and selfishness, enough so that people would think of him and say, "Jacob for Jacob for Jacob."[17] In one account, it was said that he had to lay low in Switzerland and Austria for a while, possibly marrying and deserting a woman there. By early 1895, he was back in Horrweiler and tasked with delivering several barrels of barley to Dusseldorf. Instead, he sold them off and left the country, leaving his wife and children to live with an uncle and sell what they could to cover his huge outstanding debts. A daughter took in sewing.[18]

Intriguingly, a German newspaper listing departures from January 13, 1905, mentions both a Jakob Schmidt of Horrweiler and a Jakob Huff of Steinbach, suggesting that he got the name he used in Wheeling from another emigrant.[19]

When he shed his clothes on the banks of the Ohio River, he shed the name as well. Days after his phony death, he arrived in a new city, having taken on what was likely the full name of Caroline's previous husband: Johann Adolph Hoch.

2

THE WIVES AND CRIMES OF JOHANN HOCH

In July 1895, the biggest news story in Chicago, Hoch's brand-new home, was the investigation into the "Holmes Castle" on Sixty-Third Street, a rickety building full of hidden rooms and secret passages where druggist and swindler H.H. Holmes, now awaiting trial in Philadelphia, was rumored to have killed any number of people. "Hoch" would have heard the case talked over endlessly at the saloon he purchased on Western Avenue.

He had developed an entirely different persona, as well as a new backstory. Gone was the storytelling musician of Wheeling; now, he was a brash, arrogant man with a dark sense of humor. He told one William Brenck a completely fanciful tale about his history as a chemist and soldier.

"I could do things with chemistry," he told him, "that would make your hair stand on end."

He also rambled about how awful and gullible women were: "[He said] they should be classed as domestic animals, not human beings," Brenck would recall. "Hoch was a bad man."[20]

He told another customer, Benno Lechner, that he needed a new wife, and Lechner suggested "the wealthy widow across the way." This was Marie Julia Steinbrecher, who was roughly ten years Hoch's senior, and owned $14,000 in property.[21]

Very soon after, he married Julia in the office of Moritz Kaufman, a justice of the peace who took out advertisements for his services in newspapers. Caroline Hoch Huff had been dead for only two months.

A cabinet card, taken at a studio near Hoch's saloon, of Hoch and Julia Steinbrecher. *Chicago History Museum.*

The new couple gave a wine supper, paid for with money borrowed from Lechner, and moved into an apartment on Belmont Avenue, conveniently located near the Krauspe Funeral Home. Julia took sick just a few weeks later.

"She had never been sick before," her foster son William later recalled. "Hoch sat beside her bed all the while. He would allow no one else to give her medicine. He constantly gave her a liquid in which he had mixed a white powder....Always after drinking it, my mother had cramps in her stomach....She called me to her bed one day [and said,] 'This man is not what he pretends to be. He wants to get my money. He is slowly poisoning me.'"[22] William believed she was simply delirious.

But William's wife heard the same from Julia, and when Benno Lechner visited, Julia turned to him with "a frightful expression" and said, "I believe my husband is trying to poison me." When Lechner tried to taste the mysterious medicine, Hoch grabbed his wrist and stopped him.[23]

Aware of the suspicions, Hoch limited access to Julia. The maid, Annie Ehert, began telling anyone who came to the door that Julia didn't want any more visitors while she was sick.

Julia died in early December, and the speed with which Hoch arranged the funeral disgusted William. "[She] died at six o'clock in the evening and was buried at nine o'clock the next morning by Hoch's direction," he recalled. "Hoch stripped off her rings and her earring. When the undertaker came to lay her out Hoch kept saying 'mach geschwinde' ['hurry']."[24]

Hoch hadn't wanted any neighbors at the funeral, but several came around and gossiped that Julia's death was suspicious. In some versions of the story, a man even went so far as to stop the funeral procession as it made its way to Graceland Cemetery, but Hoch produced a letter signed by the appropriately named Dr. Grimme, attributing her death to natural causes.

She was buried in an unmarked twenty-dollar grave in the northeast corner of the cemetery.[25] William would remember Dr. Grimme telling him the cause of death was gastritis,[26] though both the death certificate and cemetery records say she died from diabetes.

Julia had made out a will leaving all her property to her new husband, and when Hoch sold it off, he cleared about $4,000. He continued to live around Belmont for a while and then vanished. Annie Ehert reportedly tried to sue him for breach of promise; apparently, he had convinced her to help him keep visitors away by promising to marry her when Julia died.[27]

HOCH WAS QUOTED AS saying, "All women who are not married want to get married. The marrying mania never leaves them. From childhood they… are taught that their one great object in life is to marry well, and, if not well—why, marry anyhow."[28]

Despite the economic and social pressure for women to be married to *somebody*, finding a spouse could be a challenge. Some people took out advertisements in the matrimonial sections of newspaper classifieds, and others employed a matchmaking agency. There were over one hundred such agencies operating in Chicago around 1895, and even the most legitimate provided easy prey for swindlers.

In early 1896, Hoch met Minnie Warnke through Gustav Sterlow's employment agency, which, in most accounts, was little more than a front for a shady matrimonial agency. She claimed to be a "a widow and all alone" but with property, including a house in "a beautiful part of Chicago," just the sort of prey he was seeking. Hoch took her to Justice Kaufman's office on January 16, 1896, exactly one month after his last wife was buried. The day of the wedding, Hoch took Minnie to the Belmont Avenue house and asked her for $1,400 to pay off the mortgage on it.

But in any given arrangement made by a matrimonial agency, there was an excellent chance that the bride, the groom or the agency was up to some sort of scam. It only stands to reason that now and then, more than one party would be running a scheme. And in this case, it seems that all three were. Strelow was likely up to something, and Hoch certainly was. Minnie, for her part, was not a widow at all; she was still married to a man named Herman Domke and possibly some other men as well.

Minnie Warnke (alias Emma Rankin, Ernestine Domke, and others). *From the* Chicago American.

Details of her marriage to Hoch are murky, but it lasted only a few days at most before one or both realized that their attempt at a scam was a bust. Minnie was soon back living with her legal husband, and Hoch was seeking another bride.

In April, Hoch married Martha Hertzfeld, who had been living with her married sister, Augusta Burmeister, just above the Loop, Chicago's main downtown area.

A neighbor recalled Hoch as a devout man who "insisted on prayer and singing religious hymns morning and evening."[29] This was another entirely new persona for him, presumably one that ingratiated him to Martha.

Hoch offered to take Martha and Augusta on a trip to Germany. The day before they were to depart, he told them that the Building and Loan Association, in which they both had money saved, was probably going to fail while they were gone and that they better get their money before leaving.[30] Hoch accompanied Augusta to the bank and even held her cash for her.

On the way home, with both Martha's and Augusta's savings in hand, Hoch stopped at a store and said that he wanted to buy a book; he would meet the two at home later.

"It is needless to add," Martha would later say, "he did not come back."[31]

Augusta later said that Martha, then only thirty-three years old, went gray in forty-eight hours over the loss of her savings and husband.[32]

Instead of returning home from the bookstore, Hoch went to San Francisco. Upon arriving, he took out a matrimonial advertisement in a German paper, advertising himself as a widower with a net worth of $15,000.[33] His new landlady noted that he wore two diamond rings and went by the name Jacob Schmitt, his birth name.

The advertisement was spotted by a Bavarian widow named Barbara Bossert, described in the press of the day as "a buxom woman of about 40…a simple, confiding woman." Hoch met with her on Friday, August 21, and told her his wife had died in Chicago, where he'd owned a saloon. Now, he said, he owned the Turk Street beer hall near the boardinghouse but was lonely and eager to find a new bride.[34] After a few minutes, he declared that he was ready to marry her that very night, but Barbara insisted on waiting until morning, as Fridays were unlucky for weddings.[35]

A newspaper sketch of Barbara Bossert. *From the* San Francisco Call.

The morning after the Saturday wedding, Barbara assumed she'd be pleasing her new husband when she told him she had $1,240 in cash—not as much as the $15,000 he said *he* had but enough to show he hadn't married a poor woman who just wanted his money. However, he scolded her. Didn't she know it was dangerous to keep so much cash?[36] "If anyone knew we had this money in the house," he said, "they would murder us both!"[37]

His paranoia scared Barbara so much that she gathered the money and asked him to take it to the German Savings Bank to deposit it in her name. He agreed and left at once. Of course, instead of going to the bank, he returned to his boardinghouse, where he proposed to the landlady. Upon being turned down, he left town without even collecting his trunk. Later, the landlady found an umbrella in the trunk whose long handle concealed a dagger.[38]

Barbara's story made all of the San Francisco papers immediately, and Barbara was in no mood to play nice. "He was a German," she snapped. "They're all alike—all bad."[39]

Barbara's son later said that he dropped out of school and purchased a revolver, intending to hunt "Jacob Schmitt" down and kill him. He also said that his mother "pined away" after Schmitt, ever hoping he would return and love her. She died around 1902.[40]

FROM CALIFORNIA, HOCH WENT to Cincinnati.

Jacob Levine, who ran a McMicken Avenue grocery store in a largely German neighborhood around Mohawk Bridge, remembered the October day when a "pompous, stout, medium-sized man, wearing a silk hat and carrying a gold cane" arrived. The pompous stranger asked Levine who owned the apartment building above the grocery. Told that it was the Widow Bartels, he said, "She must be a rich woman."[41]

Clara Schiller Bartels wasn't necessarily rich, but her previous husband, thirty years her senior, had made sure she was provided for. When he died of apoplexy in 1895, she inherited an apartment building at 10 East McMicken Street, which provided a steady income, both from the rents and the lease of the grocery store on the first floor.

Hoch, now with his beard grown out and continuing to call himself Jacob Schmitt, had crafted a new regal persona. He had taken to wearing a military cape and was twirling a fancy cane that everyone would remember years later. One man said, "He carried [the cane] in a way to add to his pompous bearing. In a spell of confidence one day he showed me it was hollow."[42] The hollow cane, he said, was to smuggle diamonds from Germany. (Vague stories of Hoch being involved in shady diamond deals would come up often.) Another neighbor said, "He had peculiar eyes that pierced you through and through."[43]

A grainy surviving portrait of Clara. *From the* Cincinnati Post.

Days after "Schmitt" was told about the Widow Bartels, a radiant-looking Clara told her friend that she had a secret. "It is too good to keep," she said. "I am engaged to be married very soon. I am going to marry a man who is as pretty as a picture, and he has lots of money. He is rich in his own name, and has an estate in Germany, and gets money from there all the time. I am a lucky woman."[44]

The church was crowded for their wedding on October 7, 1896.[45]

The newly-married Schmitt opened a saloon, recalled one local paper, "with a whirl and style that caused the neighborhood to

Hoch as the "Pompous Gentleman" Jacob Schmitt, as he appeared in Cincinnati. *From the* Cincinnati Enquirer.

gasp. He put oilcloth on the saloon floor and had his barkeepers dressed in white, brass-buttoned coats, a thing unknown in that neighborhood."[46]

However, some neighbors were not impressed. They felt he was just "putting on the style" to attract women.[47]

Clara's friend said, "I don't like the looks of that man; she is getting fooled."[48] But Clara seemed thrilled to be married to a man roughly half the age of her previous husband. Another friend said, "She was all wrapped up in him. She thought he was the grandest man that ever lived."[49]

Clara's worship of her new husband continued even after she took sick soon after the wedding. Even then, she told a friend "what a good, grand husband" Schmitt was. He was bringing her a glass of wine every morning.[50] She made out a new will, ensuring that in the event of her death, everything would go to him and that he wouldn't have to put up a bond.

She may have begun to recover; neighbors said they saw her out getting a drink at the hydrant a little after midnight on January 14. But at four o'clock that morning, she died.

The cause of her death was given as gastritis, complicated by exhaustion. Her will was eight days old.

Undertakers who came to the house were greeted by the well-dressed Mr. Schmitt, who showed them an immense stock of wines and liquors in the house. He insisted they have a few drinks as they worked their trade and personally assisted in turning the body, which weighed about 240 pounds. "He was a smooth talker," said undertaker Schulte. "But I thought he was too much of a windbag. I thought it was strange he gave us so much liquor when we went to embalm his wife....Schmitt told me that he had buried one wife and one or two children, and he had a notion to blow out his brains. He said he and his wife had planned to go to Germany, where he expected a fortune of 80,000 marks."[51]

The funeral was said to be more like a wedding.

"Schmitt was a revelation as a mourner," undertaker Kuntz would recall. "He looked like a millionaire at the funeral of his wife. He wore a silk hat and carried a gold-headed cane. When the question of the grave came up, Schmitt wanted his wife buried in the Walnut Hills German Protestant Cemetery. The ordinary lots are $10 and the choice ones $12. These are near the vault and one of them was selected by me for the grave. Schmitt said that he wanted the best."

Kuntz suggested he also buy a plot beside her for himself, and Schmitt said, "God knows where I will be then."[52]

Several carriages went to the cemetery. A neighbor, Mrs. Cook, noticed Schmitt crying and told him that it would do no good to cry. Schmitt replied that he was really crying for his first wife. She rode along with him in the carriage, where he said, "Haven't I given my wife a fine funeral? I paid for it all in cash."[53]

In reality, "Schmitt" never paid the bill for the funeral at all.[54]

The doctor, the undertaker and several friends of Clara had been suspicious from the start—there was a strange blue tinge in the flesh on Mrs. Schmitt's back, which wasn't common in cases of gastritis.[55] At least one person suggested the body be exhumed right after Mrs. Schmitt died. But no formal inquiry was ever made; none of the neighbors wanted the notoriety of leading the charge for an investigation. And the embalming fluid had likely contained arsenic, covering all traces of poison.

The press later noted that after Schmitt disappeared, an attorney annexed the will and sold the remaining property.

A MRS. STETLZER, WHO knew Clara well, said Schmitt "was well liked by women, who did not see into his real heart [though] my mother could see through him like a pane of glass, and I heard her say dozens of times that he was poisoning his wife to death."

Others were less concerned about the rumors. Mrs. Cook noted that after Clara's death, lots of women called on Schmitt, and he enjoyed their company, even setting some on his lap. "He had a lot of widows running after him," Cook said. "One married woman drank some wine with him, and an hour afterward she was dead in love with him. A thin, dark woman with $7,000 called often, but Schmitt didn't like her. He said he was afraid of her. One time I saw him jump as he sat in his smoking jacket. I asked him what was the matter, and he said he thought he saw his wife's ghost."[56]

Instead of pursuing the women who came to him, Hoch went after Maria Julia Kurtz Doess, who lived in the McMicken Avenue building. Mrs. Doess had taken over management of the Mohawk Saloon when her husband, Fred Doess, died. Hoch pitched in around the bar until he won her confidence and, soon enough, her hand in marriage.

When he married her on March 23, 1897, he gave his name as John Jacob Gottfried Schmitt. For a few weeks, they lived as regular newlyweds, though he never claimed to love her and never attempted to consummate the marriage.[57] Maria Julia withdrew her money from the bank (though the president persuaded her not to withdraw *all* of it), and one story held that Hoch attempted some sort of check scheme to get the rest. Soon enough, Maria Julia began falling ill; a furniture store dealer recalled Schmitt pointing out how frail Maria Julia looked and remarking that he didn't think she'd live long.[58] Neighbors recalled that he spent a lot of time looking at maps, as though he was plotting his next move.[59]

Three weeks after the wedding, Maria Julia was recovering, and Hoch told her that a wealthy relative of his had died in Germany, leaving him a fortune. Tickets to Germany were purchased for both of them, and Maria

Julia packed up all her belongings. Hoch took the trunks to the depot, promising to return in an hour so they could go to the cemetery to take a last look at her late husband's grave before heading to Germany.[60]

But he never returned from the depot, and when Maria Julia checked her money, she found that it was all gone, along with her jewelry, her late husband's watch and two trunks' worth of clothing, which later turned up in pawn shops. When a local detective located "Schmitt" in Philadelphia weeks later, Maria Julia was too ill to go identify him.[61]

"I was left almost penniless," Maria Julia later said. "I had but sixty-five cents to my name, and only the dress and underclothes I had on my back."[62]

In addition to Maria Julia Doess's money and jewelry, Hoch took her late husband's name, as he often did. Under variations of the name "Fred Doess," he spent the next year in a flurry of short marriages. There were many stories from Cincinnati that "Schmitt" had married a woman in Philadelphia after deserting Maria Julia. One legend claimed that he spent a few days in jail after stealing this new wife's money, but in Pennsylvania, stealing from a person you were married to didn't count as theft, so he was set free.

Records do show that one Frederick W. Doess married Barbara Chuston (or Christon), a German widow, in Philadelphia in May 1897. The paperwork gives the groom's occupation as "no" and says his previous wife had died two years ago. Nothing else is known of Barbara, but this was almost certainly the Philadelphia marriage rumored in Ohio.

On July 1, 1897, "Frederick Wm. Doessa" married Maggie Koelle in Brooklyn. This time, there's clear evidence that "Doessa" was Hoch. Though Hoch filled out many sets of paperwork for weddings over his career, he always seemed to forget that such forms might ask his parents' names, and he didn't trouble himself to think of false names for them. For the wedding to Koelle, he gave his parents' names as "Eliza Weber" and "Adam," his parents' real names.

He would do this often, a quirk that would make it much easier to confirm that a given alias was really him even a century later, though no one seems to have noticed it at the time. For this wedding, he also gave his address as "69 Irving Place," a building he'd later claim to own. He would desert Maggie within a month.

Hoch was back in Chicago by August 1897, now as "Fred William Doering," and took out an advertisement describing himself as a wealthy, educated man looking for a "middle aged woman of refined tastes." The advertisement specified that any applicant must have money, so he'd know they weren't marrying him for his. The advertisement was answered by Maximiliana Sperl, who had $2,500 saved, though she worked as a housekeeper for "a well-known Chicago family." During their brief courtship, he won her over with his "polished conversation and…various little favors."[63]

He took Sperl to Milwaukee to get married at the office of Justice of the Peace Zuerner. Attorneys from the office served as witnesses. Zuerner recalled "Doering" as "a refined German…cool and self possessed." He carried a small hand satchel, which Sperl said contained "a large sum of money belonging to her." Hoch gave his parents' names as "Adam Doering" and "Elizabeth Weber."

Not long after the wedding, Sperl awoke and found her husband gone, along with her savings. She went to the police at once, but a month or so later, she was living with her sister on Bond Street in Baltimore.[64] In September, a woman at the Baltimore address, presumably Sperl, was placing advertisements in German papers for her domestic services: "Good cook and can keep house; no washing."

Hoch's fall 1897 activities are a mystery, but by winter, he had returned to New York. On December 6, 1897, he married Amanda Baertz Dickhuth in Manhattan. The officiant, Reverend Schneider, was a minor celebrity in his own right for having married more couples than anyone else in town.

Hoch gave his name as Fred Doering and his mother's name as Eliza Bartels, combining her real first name with a maiden name he borrowed from a previous wife. He deserted Dickhuth very quickly, taking $250 with him.[65]

In January 1898, Hoch married Minnie Lembke as Frederick W. Doesing.[66] She, too, met him through a matrimonial advertisement. The day they met in person, he took her to the three-story building in Manhattan at 69 Irving Place.

"This is my home," he said.

"Let us go in," she suggested.

"No," he told her. "Let's go and get something to eat first."

Over dinner, he persuaded her to go to Jersey City to marry him.[67] By the time she found out he didn't own the building on Irving Place, he had taken her money, some $900,[68] and disappeared.

In March, as Frederick William Doesing, Hoch married Lizzie Schmitz in Milwaukee in a Catholic ceremony, giving his parents' real names and calling himself a "dealer in wines" on the paperwork. Described as "stylish and pretty," Lizzie had worked as a housekeeper for one Father Holzhauer, a Catholic clergyman,[69] until his 1895 death, upon which he'd left her $300.[70] She met Hoch through a matrimonial advertisement, and he took her to an apartment in Chicago, which he'd fixed up with rented furniture that he told her he owned.

Hoch took Lizzie around Chicago, showing off all the buildings he claimed to own, and ended the tour at the Bismark Hotel in the Loop. In some versions of the story, Lizzie waited for him in a hotel room and then found that her trunk, containing her cash, had gone missing.[71] In another version, she waited for him outside, became confused when he never returned, and then went to the flat to find the furniture had been taken away. In both stories, she alerted the police at once.

And here, Hoch had made a mistake. As he'd done after other marriages in the Chicago area, he rented furniture from Frederick Magerstadt, a brother of the sheriff. When Hoch tried to sell some of the furniture he'd rented, Magerstadt had him arrested and put in jail.

Magerstadt later told a story that shortly after he'd had "Doesing" arrested, a woman—likely Lizzie Schmitz—came to him for help. From their talk, he got the impression that the man had previously married her sister, who had died soon after the wedding.[72] But Magerstadt couldn't totally understand her broken English and could do nothing to help until her absent husband was released.

In jail, Hoch alternated between the names "Martin Dotz" and "Fred Doesing." According to a German-language Chicago paper, he feigned insanity so convincingly when he was first arrested that they put him in a padded cell. Indeed, he played the role of an insane prisoner to the hilt, barking orders to imaginary soldiers. In quieter moments, he claimed to be the son of a clergyman or a Prussian artillery officer.[73]

At one point, he used a handful of soap to make it look like he was a raving madman, frothing at the mouth. The keepers assumed he was faking to get out of work and were initially afraid to approach him, but eventually, he dropped the act and was sentenced to a term in the Bridewell, the prison for minor offenses, where they put him to work making brushes.[74]

When word spread that "Doesing" was wanted for multiple counts of bigamy under a variety of names, he was the subject of newspaper articles all over the country, many of which featured portraits of him with mutton chop sideburns.

Lizzie Schmitz came to visit him in prison; in one account, she even assumed he'd be moving back in with her when his term was up.[75]

A few past victims recognized him. "That man has any number of wives living," said Augusta Burmeister, Martha Hertzfeld's sister. "He was married when he married my sister. His scheme is to make out that he has lots of money. He buys furniture from a big store on time and furnishes a flat with it. Then he advertises that he wants a wife and says he is a man of means."[76]

A sketch of "Frederick Doessing." *From the* Chicago Tribune.

Augusta was now estranged from Martha, whom she blamed for the loss of her own savings. Martha was living in Pasadena and wanted to prosecute Hoch but didn't think she had the funds to match his in court. "He had too much money," Martha later said. "And was left free to dupe all those other women."[77] Milwaukee authorities, too, said the cost of bringing all the necessary witnesses to identify to Hoch as the deserter of Schmitz and Sperl would be greater than it was worth.[78]

Doessing and an unidentified woman, possibly one of his 1897–98 wives. *From the* Chicago Chronicle.

Some victims who weren't noted now would come to light—and in more detail—in 1905, when Hoch became a sensation. But others would vanish into history, with nothing left of their story but a dusty marriage record in a forgotten file.

In September 1898, a letter came to Wheeling, West Virginia, confirming that "Jacob Huff" had not really died by suicide in the river three years earlier. According to the letter, Huff had returned to Germany, where he'd just been executed, after admitting on the gallows to having murdered seven wives. This revived talk in town that Caroline Hoch Huff had been poisoned, but no further action was taken. After all, if Jacob Huff was dead, justice had been served.[79]

Reverend Haass, though, had continued to monitor Hoch, scanning German newspapers for stories of women who had been deserted. Now he saw the stories coming from Chicago about the German bigamist "Doesing" and sent a photo to the chief of police, who confirmed that Huff and Doesing were one and the same. The prisoner had probably written the letter claiming "Huff" had been hanged himself.

Now, Dr. Ford made a statement that he'd always believed that Caroline had been poisoned,[80] and authorities announced that they would investigate at last.[81]

Caroline's body was exhumed on November 13 in the presence of Reverend Haass and several others. The coffin was opened on the spot. "The physicians found that body was badly decayed," said one paper, "and that all the internal organs, including the stomach, were gone."[82] Another said, "The body was found to be practically wasted away entirely."[83]

It was years later that Haass claimed the papers had cleaned the story up a little: "To our great consternation," he said, "we discovered that someone had been to the grave and removed from the corpse all of the internal organs of the body.…This explained the mystery of former stories that during the week of her death the grave had been tampered with. It was the opinion of all that Hoch had gone there in the night, dug up the body, and removed from it the internal organs, in order to make sure that no trace of poisoning would ever be found."[84]

Both doctors present agreed that the theft hadn't been necessary: Caroline had been embalmed with a fluid that contained arsenic, making conviction for arsenic poisoning impossible.[85]

If it was murder, it had been a perfect crime.

Hoch was released from jail briefly in 1899 but only got as far as the gates before he was re-arrested on another furniture charge and jailed again for more than a year. After his discharge in October 1900, he spent some time working as a machinist in Pullman on Chicago's far south side under his real name, Jacob Schmitt.

In the summer of 1901, under the name Jacob Adolph, he had a brief affair with a woman named Nathalie Froebel, who considered securing a divorce from her husband to marry him. But then she happened to speak about it with Benno Lechner, Hoch's old friend. "I believe that man is a scoundrel," he told her. "And he is sailing under false colors if he says his name is Jacob Adolph."

Lechner told Froebel all about Julia Steinbrecher's suspicious death, and Nathalie was astonished. The next time she saw Hoch, she mentioned Julia. Hoch turned pale and stammered when she asked him questions. He disappeared from her life that same day.

Late that fall, a year after his release, Hoch met Mrs. Elizabeth Goerk, who was about a decade older than he was and had recently been widowed by a man twenty years her senior. Now, she and two stepchildren, the adult Adolph and teenage Dora, were running a boardinghouse Mr. Goerk had left her on Eugenie Street, near Lincoln Park. Hoch began boarding there and immediately started pressing Mrs. Goerk to marry him.[86]

Elizabeth's brother, who was living in the boardinghouse at the time, would recall Hoch sobbing as he told the story of the day he was summoned back to Chicago by telegram just in time to watch his former wife die. Elizabeth asked her brother whether she should marry the man, and he told her she was old enough to decide for herself.[87]

The wedding took place in Wisconsin on November 20, 1901.

Elizabeth was interested in séances and spiritualism and encouraged her new husband to study hypnotism. He dutifully sent for a mail-order course by Dr. Harradan and even got the diploma to go with it. Hoch would later say that Elizabeth had started offering services as a spiritual medium. But she didn't seem to need psychic powers to understand that something was wrong with her new husband.

Mary Elizabeth Goerk. *From the* Chicago American.

"As soon as I fell ill," she would recall, "he asked me to let him quit his work and take care of me. I did not like the look of things, so I refused, declaring that if I did not get better soon I was going to a hospital. Then he kept away except at night, and I got well."[88]

Hoch made a show of writing a will that named Elizabeth as his heir, and then he asked her to make one of her own leaving her property to him. Already suspicious, Goerk refused again.[89]

A letter arrived, purporting to be from Hoch's parents in Germany, welcoming her into "the great Schmitt family" over twenty typewritten pages. Goerk asked her new husband why a letter from Germany had arrived in an envelope from Pullman, Illinois, and Hoch tried to explain that it had been forwarded in a second envelope.[90]

His usual tactics failing, Hoch moved right to his usual endgame: he claimed a letter had arrived saying that his father had died, and he needed to go to Germany to collect $100,000.

"He showed me this," Goerk later said, "and asked me to advance him $500, which he knew I had. I smelled a rat and refused."[91]

At the end of his rope, Hoch said he would hypnotize her into giving him the money.

"Look out, Schmitt," she said. "I am going to hypnotize *you*."[92]

At last, Hoch asked her to hand over twenty-five dollars of his wages that she'd been holding on to. This she agreed to, and Hoch took it and left, wearing one of the late Heinrich Goerk's overcoats.

He never came back.

Elizabeth's brother said she missed the overcoat more than she missed Hoch.

ON MARCH 15, HOCH appeared at the Barry and Wehmiller Manufacturing shop in St. Louis, still calling himself Jacob Schmitt.

He told the owner that he was a machinist by trade and had worked at the Pullman shops in Chicago, where he'd been a foreman in charge of fifty people.[93] He'd come to town hoping to work on the upcoming World's Fair, but those jobs were all taken. He was given a job at Barry's foundry as handyman at a wage of twenty-five cents per hour.[94]

"He was a man who could not look one square in the face," Wehmiller would say. "His eyelids twitched. [But] he proved to an industrious workman. His energy was remarkable. Likewise his conceit. He thought he could do any kind of work better than any workman in the shop."[95] "Schmitt" would be recalled for his "aristocratic ways, his picturesque profanity…his excessive nervousness" and refusal to pose in group photographs.

"Schmitt was a queer duck," recalled foreman J.W. Dawson. "I think he was crazy. He acted strange. He tried to boss the men, and put on such airs that they laughed at him. Once he told me a hard luck story and said that he had lost $20,000 in Chicago, but he rambled so in telling the story that I

Mary Becher. *From the* Chicago American.

can't remember the facts....'Schmitt's hot air' became a byword in the shop."[96]

One weekend, Schmitt said he had to go to Chicago, as his wife had died there, and lamented that it would cost him money.

At a lodge meeting, he met a widow named Mary Becher. According to her son-in-law, he told her he was a machinist from Chicago named John Schultz (a rare instance of an alias without an obvious known source). He said his wife had died and his four children lived with their aunt. Mrs. Becher was an Austrian woman about a decade older than he was. She agreed to marry him before the night was over, and they were wed on April 14, 1902, just a week later.[97]

Ella, Mary's grown daughter, said, "Every one of the family was completely carried away by his smooth talking but myself....He said he had lost [a] considerable [amount] of his fortune recently in a sewer gas explosion and that it hampered him a bit just at the time. [He and mother] attended lodge meetings together and he was pointed out as a model husband by all the women."[98]

At work, he was an entirely different person, even in name. He continued to operate there as Schmitt, though word got around that he was called John Schultz at home. His coworker Edwin Meyers recalled, "We were working at the tin machine when Bob...called to me. He says, 'Go tell Schmidty that a woman is downstairs asking for Mr. Schultz.' That's Schmidty."

Meyers had turned to "Schmidty" and said, "Hello, Schultz. A woman wants to talk to you."[99]

"Don't you call me Schultz," his coworker snapped. "I (will) beat you!" He soon calmed down, but from then on, the workers all knew to call him "Schultz" when they wanted to tease him.[100]

"He wouldn't stand for being called Schultz," Emil Andris confirmed. "Some of the boys saw him downtown once dressed like a dude. He wore a long coat and a plug hat. We laughed at that too."[101]

Things went well for Hoch around the shop; he was even made a "straw boss" with a few men working under him. But then he began to talk about organizing a union, became too much trouble, and was fired on March 14, 1903.

"He acted as though he was disheartened," Wehmiller would say, after learning of the man's other crimes. "I never saw a man take the loss of a job so hard. Perhaps the poor fellow was trying to lead a better life and atone for his former acts."[102]

The local St. Patrick's Day parade was held the day after Hoch was fired. It was a cold Sunday in St. Louis with strong winds. Hoch and Mary set out to see the parade but decided to go to the zoo instead, and they stopped on the way for a drink. After taking in a bit of beer, Mary was seized with a violent illness and taken home, where she was put to bed.

Ella learned of her mother's illness only a week into it. "Schultz was there [at the house], apparently as attentive as could be. He had prepared all the food and had been giving her the medicine that the doctor prescribed." She noted to Ella that the coffee Hoch made "tasted bitter, and was unpalatable, but she drank it because he seemed so good to her that she did not want to appear unappreciative."[103]

Ella didn't believe her mother's condition was serious and was stunned when her stepfather came to say that she had died. The cause of death was given as uremia, complicated by chronic kidney disease.

It was the way Hoch acted following Mary Becher's death that made everyone suspicious. "The day after the funeral he wore a Prince Albert coat and silk hat," recalled one man. "During the year of his marriage I never saw him intoxicated, but after his wife's death he came home in great hilarity."[104]

After getting a loan to pay the funeral bill, Hoch borrowed money from several people and quickly left St. Louis, having collected $400 from a life insurance policy he'd talked Mary into taking out and not paying the doctor.

The family remained suspicious, but the doctor noted that there were symptoms he would expect to see in arsenic poisoning that he hadn't seen in Mrs. Schultz and brushed off any suspicions. He was aware that some of the children disliked their stepfather.[105] And arsenic has no taste, so the bitter coffee was probably not a clue.

Years later, when Hoch became a sensation, a story that Mary's body would be exhumed after all spread to numerous other papers, but the coroner said that the embalming fluid the undertaker used contained arsenic so there was no use in disinterring.[106]

Once again, if it was murder, it had been a perfect crime.

Hoch returned to Chicago in 1903 and courted a southside woman named Minnie Podalski, but he became distant after he found out she didn't have any money. "Oh, he was a slick one, all right," Podalski would say.[107]

Hoch was also exchanging letters with Anna Mary Hendricks, who lived near the Bridewell. Her husband, Henry, a painter, had suffered from typhoid fever in 1902, which left him with some sort of brain damage. His frozen body was found in a ditch in Prairie View at the end of January 1903, and he was buried in a remote part of Forest Home Cemetery.

"I met [Hoch], I am ashamed to say, though a matrimonial advertisement," Anna would later say. "It was the only time I ever answered an advertisement of that sort, and I did it then only for fun. I was lonely with nothing to do, and you know the old adage, 'Satan finds some mischief still for idle hands to do.' I thought to myself, 'Here is some silly old codger advertising for a wife. I'll just answer it and fool him a bit.'"[108]

But Hoch's response was so well written that Anna became curious about this "old codger" of about forty. By the end of August 1903, he'd come to meet her. She would later describe him as "fascinating." "He is a polished and ready talker," she would say. "And is so sympathetic that a woman cannot help but like him."[109]

Hoch told Anna almost exactly the same tale he was telling Minnie Podalski at the time: he was a widower whose wife and children had all died and been cremated at Graceland Cemetery in the same year.[110] Naturally, he proposed at once, though Anna convinced him to wait a few months for the wedding—until the start of the new year.

Anna Mary Hendricks. *From the* Chicago Daily News.

Throughout the courtship, he had avoided mentioning money, except to say that he wished she didn't have any. "You know that I have much more than you," he told her, "but I'm afraid the neighbors will say, 'There's that old Schmitt. He ought to be ashamed of himself, chasing poor widows for the little property they have.'"[111]

One day that fall, he asked Anna if there was a headstone on her late husband's grave, and she said she planned to have one placed there in the spring.

"The springtime will be too late," he said. "That monument must be erected before we are married. I could never bear to have people say that I married you when your first husband's grave was still unmarked by a headstone!"[112]

He loaned her money to buy Henry a small upright marker—money she paid back.

The two were married in Hammond, Indiana, on January 2, 1904. Hoch gave his name as John Jacob Schmitt, the Anglicized version of his given name. From there, they went to 111 Watt Street (now 11119 South St. Lawrence Avenue), a Pullman townhouse where Schmitt had been boarding with a family named Cain. Mrs. Cain congratulated Anna on having won "a very kind, good husband."[113]

While they were in Pullman that day, Hoch told her that soon they'd have to go to Germany, where his father was very ill. They moved to Anna's house on the southwest side, just down Twenty-Sixth Street from the Bridewell,[114]

The house where Hoch boarded in Pullman at 111 Watt Street (now 11119 South St. Lawrence Avenue). *Photo by the author.*

and Hoch quit his Pullman job (assuming he'd ever really had one) and began to prepare for the trip.[115]

Anna was thrilled with her new husband. "There never was such a model husband as he was. He broke up my washtub, saying that I should never wash again, that he did not marry me for a laundress, but a companion, and he always insisted on helping with the house work."[116]

Days into the marriage, Hoch made his standard announcement that his father had died and that they'd need to return to the old country at once to collect his inheritance. "Liebchen ["sweetheart"], do you remember I said I wish you didn't have money?" he asked. "Now I must take that back.... We must go to Germany at once. All my extra money is invested in property."[117] She agreed to withdraw the $500 she had saved.

After they went to her bank, Hoch kept lingering in shops as though he was trying to slip away. But Anna kept with him until the next day, when he left to buy their tickets. Before he departed for the ticket office, he took her in his arms and said, "God be with you 'til we meet again." He walked to the corner and turned to give a particular sort of wave people gave in music halls when they sang "Goodbye, Dolly Gray."[118]

He never came back.

Anna, slowly realizing that she'd been robbed, began to fantasize about finding Hoch and giving him the "Dolly Gray" wave herself. Later, she noted that before he left, he'd made out a will making her his heir and left her saying, "Ta ta."

"That 'ta ta' and the will were all I got for my $500," she would say.[119] "I was a fool, and I loved him."[120]

Rather than going to Germany, Hoch spent the early winter of 1904 in San Francisco, where he wrote letters to Johanna Reichel, a Chicago widow. He'd begun suggesting marriage to her around 1902 and now he picked up the pace:[121]

> *I was a lucky man when I left you, but from the hour, the day and night have been hounded by you. Dear child, you took my heart by storm.*

While Mrs. Reichel considered the proposal, Hoch also proposed to his new San Francisco landlady. The landlady was receptive, but when Hoch found she had no money, he left without either marrying her or paying his tailor. Unaware that she'd been spurned, she wrote Hoch a loving letter urging him to hurry back and sent it to what she thought was his Chicago address but was really Mrs. Reichel's. Mrs. Reichel opened it; she couldn't read much English but recognized the word *kisses* in a letter from another woman and gave up on any idea of marrying Hoch.[122]

In April, Hoch arrived in Baltimore, where he found a job as a tinsmith. Here, he gave his name as John Schultz. He told his new boss, Mr. Plumhoff, that his wife in Germany had recently died, as had three of his children, one of whom was killed in a railroad accident before his very eyes.[123]

Mrs. Eckert, his landlady there, said, "He was a nice, quiet man…but we often commented on the way he acted. In the hottest weather, when the other boarders sat on the porch and smoked and chatted, Mr. Schultz stayed in his room, with the door closed.…He would not even eat his meals at the table, but had them sent to his room. But he was so nice and gentle that my husband and I were very fond of him."[124]

A month into his Baltimore stay, Hoch found one of his favorite sorts of targets: a widow who owned a boardinghouse. Nannie Von Klencke advertised for boarders at her home at 418½ North High Street, and Hoch arrived in June 1904. He and Nannie applied for a wedding license on July 1. A newspaper wedding announcement said that "Herr Johann Shulz" had married Mrs. Von Klencke at a Methodist church and that "a visit to the groom's parents in Germany is contemplated as a wedding tour."[125]

"I was engaged to another man," Von Klencke later said. "But he seemed to hypnotize me, and soon I was his wife."[126]

Shortly after the wedding, though, the new Mrs. Schultz began to receive letters from one "Henny Brooks," who claimed to be married to Schultz and raising his child. Hoch told her not to pay attention to such things. He may have written the letters himself, looking for a way out of a marriage that wasn't paying off like he'd hoped. Before long, he announced that a wealthy relative had died and asked Nannie if she'd loan him some money to go to Germany to claim the estate. She refused, and he left town, telling her that he was going to Philadelphia.[127]

Henny Brooks, if she existed at all, was never found.

FOR ONCE, HOCH HAD been telling the truth about where he was going.

In 1899, Richard Streicher had died of typhoid fever in Philadelphia. The next year, his widow, Caroline Hunn Streicher, began running a candy store. By 1904, she was operating a boardinghouse on Stiles Street. Hoch moved in there in late August, having reverted to the name John Schmitt and taken a job at Decker's tin shop. He impressed Mrs. Streicher by expressing his respect for women.

"Schmidt never flattered me," she would say. "He just talked common sense. There was never another man like him....I thought he would be good to me."

He told her the house wasn't good enough for her and that one day he would like to take her to Germany to give her every luxury. Streicher didn't claim to have been hypnotized, exactly, but later said Hoch had "such a masterful way that she felt as if she ought to do as he wished at all times, whether it were right or wrong."[128]

"All who met him learned to like him," she would say. "He told me that he was a widower and had four children, all of whom were dead. One day he suggested that we should go to Ardmore, where his late wife was buried, and he would show me the grave. It was an unmarked stone....After pointing it out to me he laid some flowers upon it."[129]

They were married in the boardinghouse on October 20.[130] The day after the wedding, Hoch came home from work with all his tools, saying they needed repairs. He continued to leave home during working hours but didn't return to work.[131]

Days into the marriage, Hoch surprised his new bride by telling her he wanted to start doing the cooking. He also wanted her to start drinking beer, because a glass now and then would be good for her health. But he didn't want her ordering any herself—he went to pick some up. After eating the food and drink he prepared, Caroline felt ill.[132]

Caroline had two teenaged daughters, neither of whom liked Hoch much, though he treated them with kindness. "He told us," one said, "that he wished we were small so that he could bring us up as he would his own children. My sister and I think, however, that he wished we were younger so that he could exert a greater influence over our mother."[133]

Streicher would look back and note that the sicknesses she felt that October always happened after she'd eaten or drank something Hoch gave her. "Once," she recalled, "when I pressed him to take some of the coffee he had poured out for me and which I had drunk, he said that the grounds in the bottom of it were not good for him and would not take it."[134]

Barely a week after the wedding, Hoch borrowed $200 from Caroline to claim an estate in Germany. As he'd done with Anna Hendricks and others, he said he was going off to buy the tickets and never returned.

Caroline remained sick for several months before recovering. Her daughter showed her that the letter Hoch had given her with information of his German inheritance had been mailed in Philadelphia,[135] making it clear that it was all a trick. She felt lucky to be alive, even though she'd lost $200.

Hoch may have returned a few months later; neighbors said they saw him lurking near the house in late January 1905, perhaps stopping by to see if the poison had taken effect.[136]

By that time, Hoch was officially on the run from the law, making his way from Chicago to New York. After leaving Caroline, he returned to Chicago in early November. There, he met Marie Walcker, beginning the affairs that would make him famous and end his career.

3

MARIE, EMILIE, AND BERTHA

THE SCHIPPNICK SISTERS

Marie Schippnick Walcker was known as a happy woman who "always made lots of fun." She lived most of her life in Berlin before moving to Chicago in 1902 with her older sister, Emilie Schippnick Fischer, who had been a widowed a few years before. Only one of Emilie's ten children came with her.

In Chicago, they joined their other sister, Bertha Schippnick Sohn. Marie's husband, Emil Walcker, was already in Chicago as well. But over the course of their marriage, Marie had left Emil nineteen different times, including a three-year stint a decade before during which she'd lived in the United States. She finally divorced him soon after arriving in Chicago; the divorce record paints him as a violent, drunken lout who had threatened to kill her with all sorts of implements. "[A] revolver he bought expressly for myself," she said. "He threatened my life, and was going to kill me with the oil stove. Then he wanted to strike me with an ink stand…and said he would kill me before the sun would set."[137]

Divorce testimonies of the day often told exaggerated stories in order to convince a judge to grant a divorce when there was no desertion or infidelity, but Marie's claims are given some extra weight from the fact that Emil's summons was addressed to the jail. A neighbor who'd known them in Germany and even worked with Emil in a bicycle shop confirmed her account.

After being granted the divorce, Marie took in washing for a time before buying a little candy store near Lincoln Park.

Bertha came to visit her there almost every day, along with a friend, Mrs. Knipple. But neither Bertha nor Marie ever visited Emilie, and it was later noted that Emilie hadn't been close to them in Germany, either. They'd never gotten along.

Marie Walcker. *From the* Chicago Daily News.

One day in November 1904, Bertha noticed an advertisement in the matrimonial section of the *Abendpost*, a German paper, placed by a man who said he was a widow in his early thirties, possessed of some property but no children, looking to meet a woman to be his companion.

Bertha decided that her sister ought to answer and wrote out Marie's reply herself:

> *Dear sir: in answer to your honorable advertising, I hereby inform you that I am a lady standing alone. I am forty-five years of age. I have a small business, also a little fortune of a few hundred dollars. If you are in earnest, I tell you I shall be—I may be seen at any time during the day.*
>
> *Marie Walcker,*
> *12 Willow Street*

The address, 12 Willow Street, was perilously close to Elizabeth Goerk's boardinghouse, but Hoch, now reverting to the name "Johann Hoch" after several years of other names, paid a call to the candy store to meet Marie. As he often did, he immediately showed what a help he could be by stepping behind the counter to wait on a group of children. Mrs. Knipple minded the counter and eavesdropped as well as she could while Hoch and Marie went to the back room to speak over a cup of coffee.

Hoch said he was a rich man with $8,000 in the bank. His wife had been sick for eighteen years before dying in 1902; their four children were also dead.

After a while, he asked Marie if she liked him.

"Yes," she said, "if you like me."

"I like you and you like me," said Hoch, "so we can get married then, yes?"

"If what you say is true, it's all right," said Marie.

She stepped out of the back and told her friend, "Well, [Mrs. Knipple], I am going to marry him."[138]

The next day, Wednesday, Hoch took Marie to see the cottage he'd rented at 6340 South Union Street; it was on the other side of town but an easy enough streetcar ride from her sister's house (and, it would later be noted, it was only steps from the old "H.H. Holmes Castle"). Marie came back ecstatic and told Bertha that Hoch was far richer than he'd let on before and that he planned to take her to Paris when his father died and left him another fortune. She decided she would marry him that very weekend.

Reading her divorce records, one can see why Marie was so excited. In addition to his violence, Emil had never taken care of her financially. "He never supported me," she told her lawyer. "I always supported myself by washing for others." With her new husband, there'd be no more work, no more black eyes.

On Saturday, Hoch came to the store again, entering through the back. Marie was dressing in the sleeping room and called out, "My sweetheart!"

She said she'd be out into the shop as soon as she was dressed.

"Well, you can come in," said Hoch. "Don't be ashamed; of course, I see lots of women that are not dressed, it's all right."

Marie came into the kitchen to finish dressing. She was probably already decently covered, but this marks as close as Hoch ever came, in any surviving account, to showing anything close to a sexual interest in one of his wives. (Why a machinist would see lots of women undressed was never explained; there were later some rumors that said he sometimes claimed to be a chemist who experimented with cures for menopausal discomfort.)

Hoch's cottage at 6340 South Union Avenue. *From the* Chicago American.

As soon as Marie finished dressing, she held up her money: the eighty dollars in savings that she'd taken from the bank and the seventy-five dollars she'd made in selling the store. She asked Mrs. Knipple to hold it, but Knipple didn't want the responsibility. So, Hoch took it himself.

Marie didn't think much of the church, so they were married in a civil ceremony.

The officiant described Marie, age forty-seven, as "elderly." She used her maiden name, Schippnick, not her ex-husband's name, on the paperwork.

After the wedding, they went to celebrate at Bertha's house. Hoch talked a bit about religion, presumably echoing Marie's issues with the church and claiming that he'd given lectures on the subject in New York and other cities. But Bertha didn't care about religion one bit herself and didn't bother to listen.

Hoch came back the next night to pick up Marie's dog and birds. A few days later, a week or so before Christmas, the couple happened to run into Emilie at a mutual friend's house. Marie initially declined to shake hands with her sister and stepped back from her, but Hoch insisted on being introduced.

"Let me present to you my new husband," said Marie.

"Shake hands with your sister and be friends," said Hoch. "I don't want any misunderstanding in the family."

The two did shake hands, and the three left together and made plans to meet at Christmas, though Emilie opted out of going to Bertha's house with them that night.

The Christmas plans failed to materialize. By then, Marie had taken sick.

When Bertha Sohn came to visit the couple in late December on South Union Avenue, Marie had an eruption around her mouth and complained of pains in her stomach. She was frequently running back and forth to the water closet, but she was still able to get around and drink tea. Hoch said he planned to sell a lot he owned so he could buy Marie a $100 dress. "You should also buy a dress for me," Bertha teased.[139]

Marie was still feeling sick a couple of days later when Bertha came back, but she was well enough to join in the primary activity of the evening, which was speaking ill of Emilie. Marie noted that Emilie had come to the United States with 1,000 marks but left nine of her ten children behind with only ten marks between them. Hoch used a German phrase, "raven mother." Marie agreed.

Days later, Bertha received a letter saying that Marie had gotten worse, and she came to the cottage to find that Marie looked terrible. She was taking medicine hourly, complaining of an inability to control her bodily functions and fearful pains in her throat, rectum and urethra. She also had a feeling that her body "was full of crawling ants." The diagnosis appeared to be kidney trouble.

A nurse who'd been hired, twenty-three-year-old Gussie Holzapfel, administered vaginal douches every two hours and catheters and enemas as needed, among other treatments. She was paid twenty-five dollars per week.

When Mrs. Knipple came to visit, Marie was sicker than before and speaking as though she didn't expect to recover. The medicine seemed to only be making her worse, though Hoch seemed to be taking fine care of her. "Oh, my sweetheart, did the doctor say you should have iced milk?" he asked. "Oh, of course, iced milk is better than warm for you."

Mrs. Knipple's grown daughter, who had come along, suggested that iced drinks could be dangerous, but Hoch said that they felt good on Marie's burning throat, even though she wasn't able to keep any food or drink down and was vomiting frequently.

"I want to get up and dress myself," Marie said. "I want to tell you something. Dear husband, dear sweetheart, please let me talk to Mrs. Knipple."

Rather than leave the women alone with Marie, Hoch hustled the two downstairs, saying, "She will get heart disease and die if she tries to talk too much." After going back upstairs himself for a moment, he came back and said that Marie didn't even know that the two had been there.

He accompanied them outside and said, "My wife must not have any more company. Give my regards to Bertha, my sister-in-law." And he slammed the door so hard that the house shook.

On January 2, when Emilie came to bring a picture of herself as a New Year's present, she found "a regular hospital." Marie's kidney problems had abated, but now her stomach was causing her great agony.

Hoch made a great show of feeling sorry for himself. "It is the same as with my last wife," he said. "I thought I had a healthy woman this time!"

The next day, Emilie received a note from Hoch thanking her for the picture and promising to carry it on his breast. She returned to the house the next day and noticed that Marie looked worse. She offered to stay in the house to administer some of the treatments. Though she had barely spoken to Marie in years—and had by no account ever gotten along with her—she began administering enemas and emptying the slop jars. Gussie the nurse told Hoch that Marie was getting jealous of Emilie.

Gussie, feeling that Marie was improving and that Emilie was interfering with her work, quit after six days, but she promised Hoch she would come back if Marie got worse—as long as he promised Emilie would not be there.

Emilie Fischer, as she appeared in 1905. *From the* Chicago Daily News.

One evening, when Emilie went up to the bedroom, Marie told her she was going to die. "Now you can have my husband," she said.

"Why, you are only fooling," said Emilie. "You are all right."

"No," said Marie. "I don't believe I will ever get up again."

"You are foolish. I don't want your husband."

"Well, I will be dead pretty soon, and then you can have him."

Emilie turned away, biting her lip (she later said she was trying not to cry), and Marie said, "Why are you laughing at me, you human sow? You don't know how sick I am. I am about ready to die. Well, I will be gone pretty soon, and then you can have my husband. You've got ten children, and you sure will need him. I will tell him myself he had better marry you."

Emilie went downstairs and sent Hoch up to speak to her. Minutes later, she heard Marie saying, "Go on and marry her. Marry her after I am dead."

At this, Emilie bolted into the room and said, "Is this the thanks I get for what I do for you? If it were not for your illness, I would answer you very differently. I will never cross your threshold again."

She stormed down the stairs but, moments later, came back up, noting that it was nearly midnight, too late to take a streetcar back to the north side. "If you and your husband permit, I will spend the night, but this is the last time I will ever be in your house. And I will leave at six in the morning."

Setting up to sleep downstairs, she heard Marie again saying, "Go and take her; you can have her."

Emilie finally got to sleep at 3:00 a.m., and Hoch came down at 5:30 a.m., saying Marie was worse. He went to get Dr. Reese, and when they came back, the doctor called Emilie upstairs. She found her sister "ice cold."

"*Todt*," Emilie said. "Dead."

An undertaker arrived to embalm the body, and Hoch set to work outside, throwing the bottles of medicine against the wall so they'd smash against the bricks.

As he helped Emilie take the bedsheets, Hoch began proposing to her.

The way Emilie later told the story, Hoch told her that at fifty-two, she was very old. But he had money. They could open a hotel together. He could take her to Germany to visit her children. The older ones would be making their own way by now, but the younger ones could be brought back and "Americanized." When Emilie noted that the body of her sister was still in the house, Hoch said, "The dead belong to the dead and the living to the living."

She agreed to think it over and had Hoch come to stay at her own house on North Wells, since he didn't want to be left alone with Marie's corpse, which remained on the bed.

Hoch cried on the day of the funeral, which was held in the Union Avenue house. Only three of the four pallbearers Hoch had engaged came. Mindful of Marie's position on the church, Hoch had declined to bring in a clergyman, but the undertaker said a few prayers. The carriage drove to nearby Oak Woods Cemetery, where Marie was buried in an unmarked grave.

On the ride back, he continued to tell Emilie how rich he was and how his father in Paris would die soon, leaving him $20,000. Either that day or the next, she agreed to marry him.

The two were married in Joliet two days later, with Emilie's eighteen-year-old daughter, Martha, as a witness. Hoch gave his name as "John Joseph Hock" and used his parents' real names. After the wedding, the couple went to Emilie's bank in the Loop, where she withdrew $750 to give to Hoch to settle the mortgage on the cottage so they could rent it out when they went to Germany.

The next day, Emilie went to her sister Bertha's house. When Hoch arrived there after running errands, he was stopped in his tracks by Mrs. Sauerbraugh, a friend of Bertha. "Stay back," she said. "[Bertha] is saying that you murdered Marie, and you're a swindler!"

Hoch came in, where Emilie said, "How do you look; I want you now to face my sister immediately if you are not guilty."

"I am too upset," said Hoch. He excused himself to the bathroom, where he shaved off his mustache, and then he went out the door. He went to see Johanna Reichel, making one last unsuccessful plea for her to marry him, and then boarded a train out of the city.

4
CIRCULATION WARS

It took a remarkably long time for newspapers to figure out that visual appeal was good for sales. In 1895, during the H.H. Holmes craze, papers still generally had several one-column stories spread across their front pages, rarely with headlines large enough to read from more than a few feet away and usually without any illustrations above the fold. Some papers still even covered their front pages with classified advertisements.

But at his San Francisco paper, William Randolph Hearst was taking new approaches, featuring large, eye-catching artwork and layouts on the front page. By 1900, with papers in both San Francisco and New York, Hearst was even publishing photographs, something that had been almost unknown five years before. His blaring headlines were later likened to "a screaming woman running down the road with her throat cut."[140]

Much of the Hearst papers' modern reputations as unreliable "yellow journalism" come from the smears of his rivals, not from the actual content of the papers. He may have been more likely to latch onto sex scandals and lurid crime stories than some papers were, but they were no more likely to exaggerate or sensationalize than others. And the sensational stories sold well enough to provide a budget for the best investigative journalism team in the industry. His bylines bragged of their use of a special leased wire, "the longest in the world," to transmit news from coast to coast in an instant.

In May 1900, Hearst decided that a major Midwestern paper sympathetic to William Jennings Bryan could help Bryan's bid for the presidency, and he told his general manager, Sol Carvalho, "I wish you would go out to Chicago

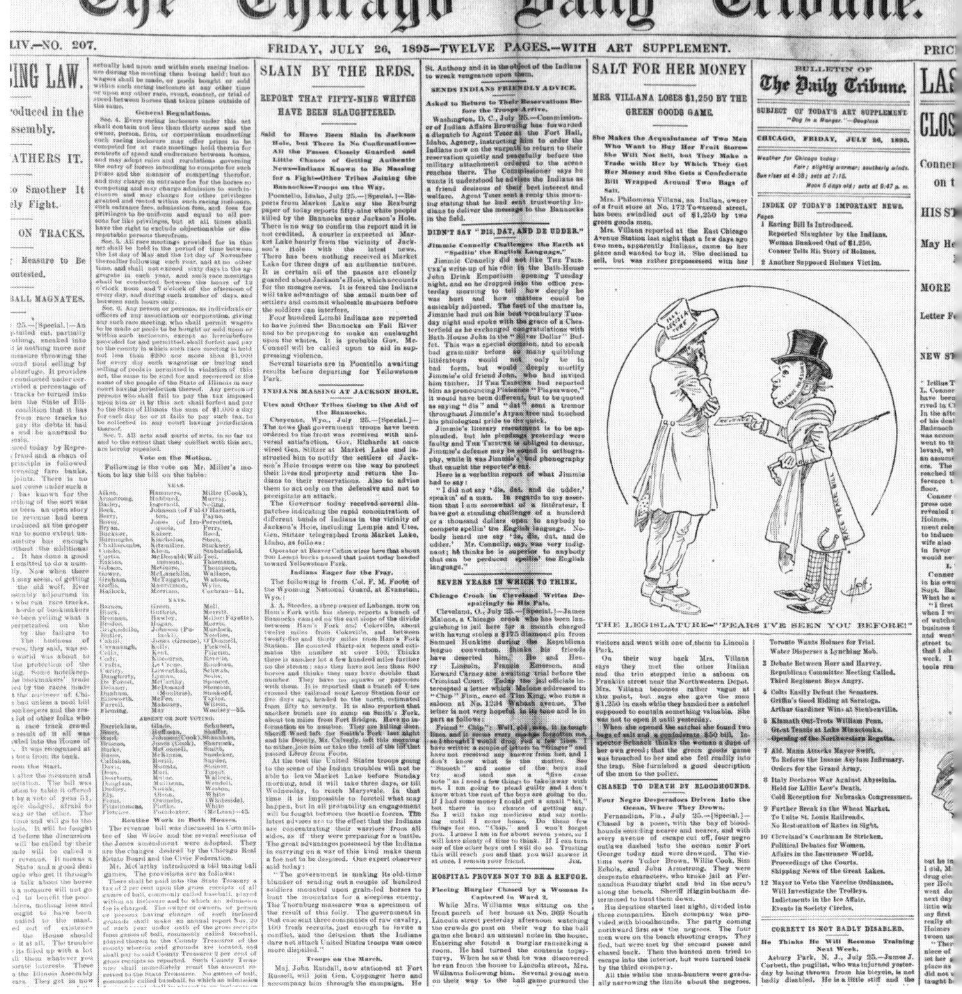

The Chicago Daily Tribune.

LIV.—NO. 207. FRIDAY, JULY 26, 1895—TWELVE PAGES.—WITH ART SUPPLEMENT.

SLAIN BY THE REDS.

REPORT THAT FIFTY-NINE WHITES HAVE BEEN SLAUGHTERED.

SALT FOR HER MONEY

MRS. VILLANA LOSES $1,250 BY THE GREEN GOODS GAME.

She Makes the Acquaintance of Two Men Who Want to Buy Her Fruit Store—She Will Not Sell, but They Make a Trade with Her by Which They Get Her Money and She Gets a Confederate Bill Wrapped Around Two Bags of Salt.

Mrs. Philomena Villana, an Italian, owner of a fruit store at No. 172 Townsend street, has been swindled out of $1,250 by two green goods men.

Mrs. Villana reported at the East Chicago Avenue Station last night that a few days ago two men, apparently Italians, came to her place and wanted to buy it. She declined to sell, but was rather prepossessed with her visitors and went with one of them to Lincoln Park.

On their way back Mrs. Villana says they met the other Italian and the trio stepped into a saloon on Franklin street near the Northwestern Depot. Mrs. Villana becomes rather vague at this point, but says she gave the men $1,250 in cash while they handed her a satchel supposed to contain something valuable. She was not to open it until yesterday.

When she opened the satchel she found two bags of salt and a confederate $50 bill. Inspector Schaack thinks the woman a dupe of her own greed; that the green goods game was broached to her and she fell readily into the trap. She furnished a good description of the men to the police.

BULLETIN OF The Daily Tribune.

SUBJECT OF TODAY'S ART SUPPLEMENT. "Dog in a Manger."—Douglass.

CHICAGO, FRIDAY, JULY 26, 1895.

Weather for Chicago today: Fair; slightly warmer; southerly winds. Sun rises at 4:38; sets at 7:15. Moon 5 days old; sets at 9:47 p. m.

INDEX OF TODAY'S IMPORTANT NEWS.

Pages.
1 Racing Bill Is Introduced.
Reported Slaughter by the Indians.
Woman Bunkoed Out of $1,250.
Conner Tells His Story of Holmes.
2 Another Supposed Holmes Victim.
Toronto Wants Holmes for Trial.
Water Disperses a Lynching Mob.
3 Debate Between Horr and Harvey.
Republican Committee Meeting Called.
Third Regiment Boys Angry.
4 Colts Easily Defeat the Senators.
Griffin's Good Riding at Saratoga.
Arthur Gardiner Wins at Steubenville.
5 Klamath Out-Trots William Penn.
Great Tennis at Lake Minnetonka.
Opening of the Northwestern Regatta.
7 Ald. Mann Attacks Mayor Swift.
To Reform the Insane Asylum Infirmary.
Orders for the Grand Army.
8 Italy Declares War Against Abyssinia.
Held for Lillie Low's Death.
Cold Reception for Nebraska Congressmen.
9 Further Break in the Wheat Market.
To Unite St. Louis Railroads.
No Restoration of Rates in Sight.
10 Cleveland's Coachman Is Stricken.
Political Debates for Women.
Affairs in the Insurance World.
Proceedings of the Courts.
Shipping News of the Great Lakes.
12 Mayor to Veto the Vaccine Ordinance.
Will Investigate the Trolleys.
Indictments in the Ice Affair.
Events in Society Circles.

THE LEGISLATURE—"'PEARS I'VE SEEN YOU BEFORE!"

CHASED TO DEATH BY BLOODHOUNDS.

Four Negro Desperadoes Driven Into the Ocean, Where They Drown.

Fernandina, Fla., July 25.—[Special.]—Chased by a posse, with the bay of bloodhounds sounding nearer and nearer, and with every avenue of escape cut off, four negro outlaws dashed into the ocean near Fort George today and were drowned. The victims were Tudor Brown, Willie Cook, Sim Echols, and John Armstrong. They were desperate characters, who broke jail at Fernandina Sunday night and hid in the scrub along the beach. Sheriff Higginbotham determined to hunt them down.

and start a paper.…We ought to be able to have the first issue on the streets by the Fourth of July."

To launch a paper from scratch in six weeks was an absurd proposition, but Hearst thrived when he was doing something that anyone else would have thought was absurd.

"It's a tough town," Carvahlo said. "We'll have to shoot our way in."

"Take all the ammunition you need," Hearst replied.[141]

Both men meant this entirely literally. To ensure prime space on the newsstands or positions on the busiest corners for their newsboys, several

All the News of All the World

CHICAGO AMERICAN NIGHT EXTRA

WEATHER INDICATIONS—FAIR AND WARM.

VOL. V., NO. 120—P. M. SATURDAY. CHICAGO, NOVEMBER 19, 1904. SATURDAY. PRICE ONE CENT.

WHO HIRED "DEATH" AUTO 278-AT THE AUDITORIUM?

POLICE SCOUR THE COUNTRY FOR MURDERER OF CHAUFFEUR

SLAIN CHAUFFEUR'S BODY AS FOUND IN AUTO OF TYPE SHOWN; MAP OF VICINITY

WHO IS THIS MAN? IS HE AUTO MURDERER?

The man, supposedly the one who ordered the auto over the Auditorium 'phone and who gave his name as "Dove," is described as follows by Lee Starks, doorman at the Auditorium Hotel:

Height, 5 feet, 6 to 7 inches.
Weight, 140 pounds.
Age, 22 to 24 years.
Hat, black derby.
Smooth-faced, dark complexioned.
Walked very erect.
Carried a suit case.

Girl Brought Into Case by Discovery of Letters in Victim's Pocket.

WILLIAM BATE, ACCORDING TO THE POLICE, MAY HAVE BEEN MURDERED BY A JEALOUS RIVAL, WHO HIRED HIM TO DRIVE AN AUTO FOR HIM AND SHOT HIM DOWN FROM BEHIND. THE THEORY WAS STARTED BY THE DISCOVERY OF TWO LETTERS AND A PHOTOGRAPH IN THE MURDERED MAN'S POCKET. BOTH LETTERS WERE WRITTEN BY THE SAME GIRL AND ONE WAS ADDRESSED TO HIM AND ONE TO ANOTHER MAN. THE PHOTOGRAPH WAS GIVEN TO BATE BY THE GIRL. THE VICTIM'S FATHER HAS GONE TO LEMONT TO GET THE LETTERS AND PICTURE.

Detectives of three cities—Chicago, Joliet and Lemont—are searching the country for twenty-five miles around Lemont for clews to the strange mystery surrounding the murder of William Bate, 1562 Kenmore avenue, chauffeur for the Dan Canary Company, who was found murdered in his machine two and one-half miles from Lemont on the Archer road early to-day.

That the man was shot down from behind as he drove his car is certain. Detectives are bending every effort to find "Mr. Dove," who summoned the auto to the Auditorium Hotel at 9:20 o'clock last night and, leaping hurriedly into the car, rushed away.

SLAYER, IT IS THOUGHT, CAME FROM A BANQUET.

No "Mr. Dove" was registered at the hotel, but the man who leaped into the big blue touring car wore full evening clothes, carried a tan suit case and seemed in a great hurry. Hotel employes declare that he apparently came from a banquet then in progress in the hotel.

Here are the theories advanced by the police:

That Bate was murdered by "Dove" after a quarrel over the payment for the rent of the machine. "Dove" objected to the price when he first rented the car by telephone. The tracks of the machine show that it flashed through Lemont and went toward Joliet. The machine turned around three miles from Lemont and started back, running nearly a mile before Bate was shot down.

That Bate was slain by farmers with whom he had an altercation in the road and that his passenger fled or was also killed.

SECOND AUTO SUSPECTED OF AIDING SLAYER.

That Bate was shot by persons riding in another automobile.

Continued on 3d Page, 5th Column.

CONSUL CARL BUENZ ILL IN NEW YORK

New York, Nov. 19.—Carl Buenz, the German Consul General at this port, formerly of Chicago, is dangerously ill. ...

ONE KILLED IN MINE EXPLOSION

Carbondale, Ill., Nov. 19.—In an explosion at the Peter Jeffery mine at Johnston City one Italian was instantly killed and two others wounded, one seriously.

The accident occurred at the time powder was being distributed to the different rooms and resulted, so it is claimed, from carelessness by the men who were handling the explosive.

The mine is a new one, having been opened but a few months.

STRATHERN RULED OUT OF GAME; MINNESOTA TEAM IS CRIPPLED

Special to the American.

Marshall Field, Nov. 19.—Moses Strathern, Minnesota's captain, was ruled out of the game to-day at the last minute.

The protests sent to Dr. Williams by the Northwestern authorities carried evidence so indisputable that Williams ordered Strathern to the side lines. His absence from the center of the Gopher forwards weakened the ...

BLACK HAND VICTIM

A front page of the *Tribune* from 1895, during the H.H. Holmes sensation, versus a fall 1904 front page of the *American*. *From the* Chicago American.

of the Chicago papers employed "sluggers" who were known to get violent. The *Chicago Chronicle* said that they didn't participate in such things, of course, but that other papers "maintain regular schools for crime…[and] graduates thugs, holdup men, and murderers" to get their circulation up.[142] These "graduates" became a minor-league team for the underworld. Future gangsters Mossy Enright and Spike O'Donnell both made the news as "sluggers" in their salad days.

There were about a dozen major daily papers in Chicago at the time—some published in the morning, some in the afternoon. As he always did in a new town, Hearst had his men buy up top talent from other papers. This time, he poached Max Annenberg, the *Tribune*'s circulation manager, who brought along and expanded his "wrecking crew." According to the *Chronicle*, "The Hearst paper…went to such places as Harry Gilmore's boxing school on Clark Street and signed as fierce a bunch of young pugilists as probably were ever gathered together under one management."[143]

The paper launched on July 2, 1900. As a publicity stunt, William Jennings Bryan sent the message "Start the Presses" over the wire from New York to Chicago, and newsboys were running with the first issue only minutes later.

By 1905, the new paper, *The Chicago American*, was a well-oiled machine that had changed the face of newspapers in the city. Their illustrated front pages had headlines in fonts stretching to 480-point sizes and were occasionally even printed in red ink—sometimes because the news warranted red letters and sometimes just to liven things up (one headline that used red ink was "Lincoln's Birthday Celebrated").

Hearst believed that women reporters brought in women readers, so he employed several, often giving them individual bylines (which few reporters got at the time) and generally without such dismissive sobriquets as "Our Little Girl Reporter," which other papers would continue to use for decades. Winifred Sweet, Hearst's star writer in San Francisco, said years later that Hearst was "the best boss, the kindest friend, and the simplest-hearted, wisest, most understanding, most forgiving, most encouraging human being it has ever been my luck to know."

Of course, these women reporters didn't exist without criticism. In one speech at the Chicago Auditorium, John Alexander Dowie, the faith healer and founder of the town of Zion, Illinois, denounced two reporters, Jean Cowgill of the *Chronicle* and Evelyn Campbell of the *American*, as "creatures of the devil, sent to Earth on purposes to overthrow [my] few acres of heaven."

Both Cowgill and Campbell would go on to play major parts in the story of Johann Hoch.

THE CHICAGO DAILY NEWS.

SPORTING EXTRA

LIEUT. RICE RACE WINNER

GAINS AND LOSSES OF CHICAGO NEWSPAPERS FOR 1904.

AS TO CIRCULATION.

AS TO ADVERTISING.

CHICAGO DAILY JOURNAL

CANAL BODY GIVES AWAY FORTUNES

MOBS CRY TO CZAR, 'MERCY OR WE DIE!'

WIFE DEAD 2 DAYS, MAN WEDS SISTER

LICENSE AND POLICE HALLS

CASTRO OUT WITH U. S.

THE CHICAGO EVENING POST.

HONOR MOTHERS AMID OUTLAWRY

SMOOT ON THE STAND

DEATH IN A MYSTERY.

AFTER RAILROADS AND STATE BOARD

SPORTING EDITION CHICAGO AMERICAN SPORTING EDITION

POLICE DEMAND TO DIG UP DEAD BRIDE'S 9-DAYS' BURIED BODY

WAS SHE KILLED? ? ? ? IF SO, BY WHOSE HAND?

LATEST NEWS

LATEST RACING RESULTS

RUSSIAN TROOPS CALLED OUT TO QUELL RIOTS NOW SPREADING IN CZAR'S DOMAIN

LIEUTENANT RICE WINS SECOND RAC

A montage of evening papers from January 20, 1905, the day the Hoch story broke. *Author's collection.*

Hoch became a sensation due to the diligence of the *Chicago American*'s city editor, Moe Koenigsberg. He often scanned new wedding and burial permits to get story ideas, and one winter's day, he noticed the name "John Hoch" among the burial permits. The name alone "suggested neither romance nor drama," but he felt as though it rang a bell and assigned a reporter to see if there was anything in the story.

Or, anyway, that was how Koenigsberg told it years later. It's more likely that he got a tip from one of many local officials, such as coroner's deputies, whom the paper had on retainer for scoops. The *American* had a vast network of officials, bellboys, waiters, switchboard operators, nurses and others who were paid for good tips.[144]

In any case, reporters began to investigate this man who had married Marie Walcker, buried her, and then married her sister and vanished. By the end of the day, Inspector George M. Shippy had decided to exhume Marie's body from her grave.

Koenigsberg wrote of this only decades later, when lots of veteran reporters were writing potboiler memoirs in which they took credit for causing or inventing nearly everything that ever happened. Many of their "memoirs" were tall tales, far less reliable than the actual reporting had been. But the papers published on January 20, 1905, largely confirm Koenigsberg's claims of breaking the story. Reporters that day were able to put the basics of the story together in time for the evening papers, barely twenty-four hours after Hoch disappeared. The *Chicago Daily News* gave the story a small mention. A small *Journal* headline read "Wife Dead 2 Days, Man Weds Sister." The *Post* gave it the slightly more lurid but still small headline: "Death in a Mystery." All of these were mixed among stories about Czar Nicholas and local sports that got equal or greater space.

The *American* would outdo them all. It ran at least three editions with the story on the front page that night, all with "screaming down the road with her throat cut" headlines. Though none of the other papers had photographs to go with the story yet, the *American* had a large portrait of Emilie Fischer and a smaller, older picture of Marie, her short hair severely parted down the middle. They had already secured interviews with Dr. Reese, nurse Gussie Holzapfel, Bertha Sohn, and Emilie herself.

Dr. Reese said, "There was nothing suspicious about the death. I never heard any question until an hour ago from the coroner's office."

Bertha Sohn seemed baffled to contemplate the month she'd just lived through. "He was the smoothest talker I ever saw," she said. "He was fascinating."[145]

The other papers had many of the same quotes, so it's hard to know who *really* got the scoop. But it's certain that the *American* treated it like a major story first.

5

THE STORY UNFOLDS

By the time the morning papers—*The Tribune*, *The Chronicle*, *The South Side Sun* and *The Daily Inter-Ocean*—hit the stands on January 21, they'd had time to clear up the timeline a bit, and there were more photos. No one had found a picture of Hoch himself yet, but by the evening, the *American* even had a murky picture of Marie's now-empty grave. She had been exhumed already.

After the coffin was thawed, the lid was lifted at a coroner's physician's office for Marie's sisters to identify the body. Bertha fainted, but Emilie simply said, "Yes, that is Marie."

The doctors saw no external sign of poisoning; the *Inter-Ocean* even put "No Poison" in its next headline. But Inspector George M. Shippy kept saying that this may be "another H.H. Holmes case."

Shippy was, to say the least, an odd duck. Only weeks before, Shippy had rented a horse that was thought to have been ridden by a murdered man to see if it would magically take him to the killers. It didn't work. Days later, he reportedly propped up the murdered man's body in the receiving vault at Mount Carmel Cemetery. One by one, suspects were led into the vault, where Shippy hoped the guilty party would be scared into confessing. That didn't work either.

Now, he rushed right into making grand claims about Hoch. "I now know of twelve living wives of this man," he told the *Daily News*, "and at least four who have died."[146]

HOCK, DEAD BRIDE'S WIDOWER, WED 20 WOMEN, POLICE THINK

Wholesale Marriage Swindles Laid to Husband of the One Whose Body Is Exhumed on Sister's Charge of Murder.

Twenty marriages to women in different parts of the United States are being traced

Was Mrs. Marie Hoch Poisoned? Chemical Analysis of her stomach to-morrow is to determine.

EXHUMING BRIDE'S BODY: ACTORS IN TRAGEDY.

At the top is shown Mrs. Marie Hock in the bridal robe she wore at her marriage to Johann Hock. Her body was exhumed yesterday. Below is Mrs. Emily Hock, who made the revelations which resulted in the search for the suspected husband. In the middle is a photograph taken by a staff photographer, showing the coffin containing the bride's body being raised.

by Inspector George M. Shippy, who expects to lay them at the door of Johann Hock.

Hock's latest matrimonial ventures, in which he married one sister, buried her

PROVE HARLAN FOE OF PUBLIC CONTROL

BOYCOTTED EDITOR OF LIFE-BARRED FROM THEATER

All the News of All the World

CHICAGO AMERICAN NIGHT EXTRA

WEATHER INDICATIONS—SNOW FLURRIES.

VOL. V., NO. 174—P. M. SATURDAY. CHICAGO, JANUARY 21, 1905. SATURDAY. PRICE ONE CENT.

POISON SEARCH IN MYSTERY OF DEAD BRIDE

Hoch, Missing Husband, Is Blamed by Police for Succession of Crimes.

In the presence of Coroner Hoffman, Deputy Coroner Buckley, Police Inspector Shippy and two detectives, a post-mortem examination of the body of Mrs. Marie Hoch was begun this afternoon by Coroner's Physician Lewke, searching for traces of poison the police believe will be found when the mystery of the bride's death is dispelled.

At the same time detectives detailed by Inspector Shippy were hard at work on information which he believes will connect Hoch with a series of matrimonial adventures in which robbery was the motive, and in some of which murder played a part.

The body of the first Mrs. Hoch was exhumed at Oakwood Cemetery on a court order issued by Judge McEwen and removed to the undertaking rooms of P. C. O'Donnell, 6329 Cottage Grove avenue.

Body Is Frozen.

Leaves With Her Cash.

Death Plot Suspected.

Seeks Warrant for Hoch.

Continued on 4th Page, 1st Column.

OPENED GRAVE OF MRS. MARIE HOCH AT OAKWOODS CEMETERY.

Photograph by Chicago American staff photographer.

In the presence of police, detectives and physicians from the office of the County Coroner, the body of Mrs. Hoch, which was dug from the grave shown in the picture, will be examined to establish a clew in the mystery of her death. This picture shows the grave at Oakwoods, which was dug open to-day by the custodian of the cemetery.

MOBS LOOT SHOPS MANY HURT IN FIERCE FIGHTS DEFY CZAR'S TROOPS

Special Cable to the American.

St. Petersburg, Jan. 21.—Mobs forced an entrance to several of the factories run by loyalist employers, which are still in operation to-day, and, after attacking the workmen and severely maltreating them, began to smash the machinery. Thousands of rubles' worth of property was destroyed. The police were powerless to cope with the frenzied men, and the presence of troops in other parts of the province made them bold and desperate. Bricks and stones were freely thrown and several persons were hurt.

Thousands of strikers, Socialists and students meanwhile paraded the streets, shouting:

"WE WANT NO MORE WAR!"

Inflammatory placards were borne on shoulders reading:

"DOWN WITH TYRANNY!"

"WHAT IS MANCHURIA TO US!"

LAWYERS NEAR FIST FIGHT AT INGA HANSON'S TRIAL

CHICAGO BANDIT'S "BOMBS" ARE STUFFED WITH SAWDUST

WOMAN WHOSE BODY WAS DISINTERRED.

Opposite: A photo said to be of Marie Walcker in her wedding dress, with officials, including Inspector Shippy, exhuming her coffin. A portrait of Emilie Fischer can be seen below. *From the* Chicago American.

Above: The opened grave and a more recent photo of Marie. *From the* Chicago American.

Later that day, he told the *Sun* and *Tribune* that Hoch had married at least *twenty*. "I don't wish to do the man an injustice," he added, "but the facts are that ten of his wives have died mysteriously."

Anna Hendricks, Hoch's early 1904 wife from his time in Pullman, went to the police that day. After touring the Union Avenue house, she noted that the large shoes must be his because his feet had been disfigured by bunions. Police knew at once she was really a Hoch victim, as that was a detail they'd kept from the press. They were interested to hear that she'd been working nearby at 5912 South Union Street, and they were especially interested when she said that when Hoch deserted her, he'd been talking about moving into an apartment in a building he claimed to be part-owner of at 703 Sixty-Third Street. She may not have realized that that was the old H.H. Holmes "Castle," but the police surely did.[147]

That Hoch was somehow connected to H.H. Holmes, the murderer who'd filled papers a decade before, became a part of the story almost instantly.

Hoch's Union Avenue cottage, after all, was barely a block from the castle building. The *Chicago Sun*'s large headline on January 21 read, "Like H.H. Holmes Case," and two days later, as more rumors spread, the lead article screamed, "Was Holmes' Janitor." Shippy bluntly told the *American*, "I regard [Hoch] as an even greater criminal than H.H. Holmes, for whom he worked as a janitor in the Holmes Castle."[148]

It was an angle that would come up again and again, fooling even the best reporters.

6

EVELYN CAMPBELL'S QUEST

For the next few days, front pages of the papers would alternate between stories of the violent revolution in Russia and new information about Johann Hoch. The number of Jews massacred and Hoch wives swindled climbed in edition after edition. Pictures of Hoch himself—his Bridewell mug shot and his wedding photo with Julia Steinbrecher—were finally published January 23.

Newspaper articles of the day were essentially a group effort, especially at the *American*. Carvalho had reasoned that no reporter possessed the skills to gather facts and write stories in equal measure; now that telephones were everywhere and Mr. Hearst's money was funding a seemingly infinite staff, the same person didn't have to do both. "Leg men" would gather data, and they'd call it in to the "rewrite" men.

One *American* reporter who did do both was Evelyn Campbell, one of the reporters who had been called a "creature of the devil" on the stage of an auditorium. Koenigsberg recalled her as "my star sob sister," though that widely scorned term for women reporters wouldn't become common for some time after her tenure. "Not only [was she] an indefatigable worker, but she flashed more journalistic fire than any of the men on the staff. In the stress of an unfolding yarn, she made light of food and rest. It was not unusual for her to snatch a few hours' sleep on a pile of exchanges in the newspaper morgue."

Often, one of Campbell's articles would appear in several editions per day. Comparing the changes between versions shows that the rewrite desk

Various newspaper copies of Hoch's Bridewell mug shot, which was finally published days into the manhunt. Most papers had a version close to the one on the left, though the slimmer-looking version may be closer to the lost original. *Author's collection.*

would edit her work as needed to fill space or reflect new information gathered between editions, but she seems to have done most of the writing herself. Once, while reporting on a girl accused of sending obscene letters in Mendota, Illinois, she walked into the Western Union office and asked if they could telegraph a five-thousand-word dispatch to her paper. The operator was busy and seemed hesitant, so she said, "Well, get up and let me have the key." And she did it herself.[149]

Most newspaper writers didn't get a byline in those days. Evelyn usually did. Often, she even had her picture printed next to the column. Sometimes the articles were even credited to her real name, Nana Springer.

Born in 1874, one profile read that "in the cradle she was picked up by a feminist relative. Her mother promptly snatched her back, but apparently too late."[150] That same mother educated her at home through high school, an education that barred any fiction. After a stint at teaching school, she wrote for a Wisconsin newspaper before going to work for the *American*.

In the fall of 1904, she covered an Episcopal minister's conference, a high-profile suicide, and the elopement of a young woman who wished to escape her parents. She interviewed experts about whether playing with toy soldiers made children cruel. Most intensely, she covered the trial of Victor Roland O'Shea, who was accused of murdering a young woman whom he'd secretly wed. She interviewed O'Shea's family, analyzed his love letters, and reported on Clarence Darrow's defense in court.

A restored profile view from the Bridewell mug shot. *Author's collection.*

She made her entry into the Hoch case on January 25, landing what appeared to be a feature interview with Emilie Fischer.

"It was for *mein kinder* I married him," Fischer told Campbell. "He promised me we should go back to Germany and get mein kinder. And now—ach gott!"

Exactly how the interview was conducted is not known—presumably there was a translator—but Campbell was likely the first woman to speak to Fischer about the case. "Seven years ago, my husband, William Fischer, died in Germany," she said before listing the ages of her children. "I came to America, thinking I could make money faster here and get the most of them with me again."

She admitted she'd never been on good terms with Marie. After reciting the story of the dying Marie accusing her of wanting Hoch for herself, she said that Hoch had first spoken of marriage while she was dressing the body.

"It seemed too good to be true. I knew that I was doing no wrong to my sister, for she did not love Hock. She married him in a business way, just the same way I did. And I wanted my children so much."

Campbell met with Shippy to find out everything he had on Hoch and said that her hours with him were "the most absorbing I ever spent."

"He is a regular Dr. Jekyll and Mister Hyde, isn't he?" she asked the inspector.

"That character of fiction wasn't a marker to reality," Shippy told her. "Neither could [H.H.] Holmes…come anywhere near this man in the diabolical way he carried on his work."

He showed Evelyn a letter, not yet known to the public, from an informant who claimed to be able to tie Hoch to more marriages and perhaps even to another murder.

"He appears to be a man of unlimited daring as well as one of much ability," Shippy said. "I think he got his training in the school of Holmes, the archfiend of the sixty-third street castle, but he outdistances Holmes in cleverness at every turn."

In her column, Campbell promised to stay with the story. Her excitement was palpable: "I have arranged," she told her readers, "to help in the solving

Two of the photos that accompanied Evelyn Campbell's articles, one of which used her real name, Nana Springer. That reporters used pen names was not a secret; various statements suggest that Springer thought of "Evelyn Campbell" as a sort of secret identity, a whole persona she could become when using that name. *From the* Chicago American.

of the problem, the greatest criminal puzzle with which the police have had to deal for some time. Day after day I shall follow this clew [*sic*] through the labyrinth to which even my inexperienced eyes can see it will lead. What I find out I will tell to you each day."

She closed with a plea for help.

"You, some of you, can help me in this work," she wrote. "If you ever knew Hoch or anyone under a different name you think was he, will you not write to me detailing the circumstances?"

Evelyn Campbell was now a part of the story—and so were her readers.[151]

SHIPPY'S MYSTERIOUS LETTER WAS a tip from Gustav Strelow, saying that they should speak to Hoch's second Chicago wife, Minnie Warnke, alias Ernestine Domke (who was currently going by Minnie Rankin).

Upon being brought in for questioning, Minnie said, "I do not know Mr. Hoch, and I never heard of him."

Detective Miller showed her the anonymous letter naming her. She grabbed it and tore it to pieces and then broke down and admitted that she'd *known* Hoch, but she still insisted she hadn't married him.

She said she'd met Hoch through Strelow's agency around 1896. In the version of the story she told now, she'd become suspicious after this new acquaintance asked to borrow money from her. She had even surreptitiously removed the bullets from a revolver Hoch carried. Three days later, he'd pointed it at her, saying, "Now you must give me all your money, or I will shoot your head off." She told him she'd go to the bank and then ran away.

"I heard him snapping the revolver at me," she told them. "I never saw him afterwards."[152]

The police seemed to doubt the details (it certainly wasn't how Hoch normally acted) and confronted her with bits of her own history. In 1897, the year after her time with Hoch, Warnke had been accused of the unsolved murder of Ernest Keuneth, an old man who'd been hacked to death with a corn knife in 1892.

Warnke had been a housekeeper for Keuneth's next-door neighbor at the time of his death, and police had no suspects in the case until Warnke's husband, Herman Domke, came to them and named his wife as the killer. He also said that around of the time of the Keuneth murder, she had burned sulfur in the chimney, and the fumes had fatally suffocated a child who lived in the apartment upstairs.[153] Herman even claimed that Minnie had offered to murder his children from a previous marriage if he took out life insurance on them.

Warnke had lingered in jail for two weeks, during which she stayed in the news by feigning insanity. But there wasn't enough evidence to put her on trial in the end. Herman's accusations were *probably* the result of a bitter divorce case, in which each accused the other of attempted murder. But Warnke's adult son, Robert Rankin, who had been living on his own since the age of thirteen, admitted his mother had once asked him to take Herman out in a boat and kill him. He'd assumed she was fooling at the time, but now, he wasn't sure.[154]

Mindful that she could be charged with bigamy herself, having still been married to Domke during her time with Hoch, Minnie continued to deny the marriage.

7
LIKE ZITHERS FOR HIM

Days into her coverage, Evelyn Campbell wrote, "The mystery of this man's character grips me with its weird fascination as I get deeper and deeper into the labyrinth."[155] The *American* was running advertisements asking, "Are You Following Miss Campbell's Hock Clews? The Detectives Are." (They were still usually spelling his name as "Hock," and "clew" would persist as the preferred spelling in newspapers for years.)

The advertisement was probably correct. Evelyn was likely getting just as many leads as Shippy, if not more. Many people with vital information may have felt safer going to her than to the police. Others simply knew they were more likely to get a reward from the paper than from the authorities.

In her column for January 26, Campbell detailed what she'd learned when she'd gone to interview witnesses.

"All day long I tramped the snowy streets," she wrote, "visiting first one and then another of the women whom an unkind fate has thrown in the way of the suave, smiling devil…these weary, sad-eyed women who were either themselves duped…or stood helplessly by and watching him gain and betray the confidence of sisters or mothers they loved."

One tale she came across frequently said that Hoch had charmed women with his skills as a musician.

"He was a splendid player on the zither," an unnamed witness said. "And I guess women were like zithers for him."

Evelyn described that quote as jumping out at her like light in the darkness. "As clearly as if he stood before me, I saw how this man had swept the

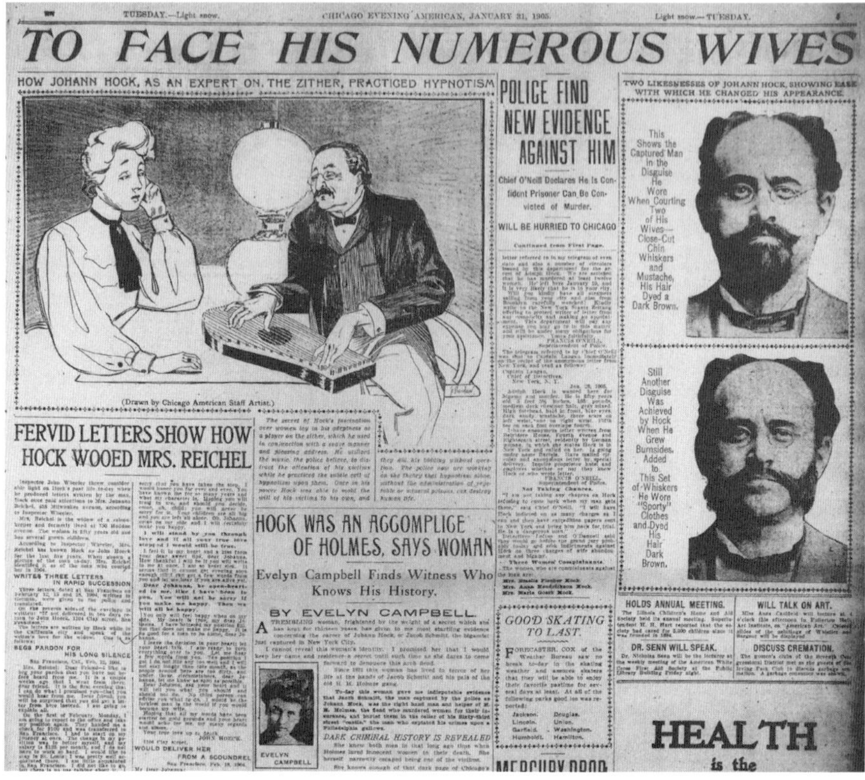

TUESDAY.—Light snow. CHICAGO EVENING AMERICAN, JANUARY 31, 1905. Light snow.—TUESDAY.

TO FACE HIS NUMEROUS WIVES

HOW JOHANN HOCK, AS AN EXPERT ON THE ZITHER, PRACTICED HYPNOTISM

(Drawn by Chicago American Staff Artist.)

POLICE FIND NEW EVIDENCE AGAINST HIM

Chief O'Neill Declares He Is Confident Prisoner Can Be Convicted of Murder.

WILL BE HURRIED TO CHICAGO

Continued from First Page.

TWO LIKENESSES OF JOHANN HOCK, SHOWING EASE WITH WHICH HE CHANGED HIS APPEARANCE.

This Shows the Captured Man in the Disguise He Wore When Courting Two of His Wives—Close-Cut Chin Whiskers and Mustache, His Hair Dyed a Dark Brown.

Still Another Disguise Was Achieved by Hock When He Grew Burnsides, Added to This Set of Whiskers He Wore "Sporty" Clothes and Dyed His Hair Dark Brown.

FERVID LETTERS SHOW HOW HOCK WOOED MRS. REICHEL

WRITES THREE LETTERS IN RAPID SUCCESSION

BEGS PARDON FOR HIS LONG SILENCE

WOULD DELIVER HER FROM A SCOUNDREL

HOCK WAS AN ACCOMPLICE OF HOLMES, SAYS WOMAN

Evelyn Campbell Finds Witness Who Knows His History.

BY EVELYN CAMPBELL.

A TREMBLING woman, frightened by the weight of a secret which she has kept for thirteen years, has given to me most startling evidence concerning the career of Johann Hock, or Jacob Schmitt, the bigamist just captured in New York City.

EVELYN CAMPBELL

DARK CRIMINAL HISTORY IS REVEALED

GOOD SKATING TO LAST.

HOLDS ANNUAL MEETING.

DR. SENN WILL SPEAK.

WILL TALK ON ART.

DISCUSS CREMATION.

HEALTH is the

A *Chicago American* sketch of Hoch playing a zither, with an Evelyn Campbell article and doctored versions of the Bridewell photo to show how Hoch might have disguised himself. *From the* Chicago American.

heartstrings of the poor, plain women he married and struck the melody of love and trust from their souls, even as his practiced fingers brought harmony from the strings of the zither."

She also heard many stories of Hoch demonstrating that he was good with housework. "These women had been used to fathers, brothers, husbands, and sons who thought of home only as a place in which to eat and sleep and of the women of the house only as household drudges."

And yet she also determined that Hoch was most successful when approaching marriage as a business: "He did not profess romantic love for a woman whom he had known but a few days.…He made his proposal of marriage in a calm, businesslike manner which appealed to these practical, hard-working women."

Though sensationalism sold papers, as the number of reported wives climbed higher and higher, Evelyn noted that most of the women who claimed to have been duped by Hoch were surely mistaking him for someone else. It was clear that he wasn't the only person out in the world pulling these sorts of tricks. She noted that many of the stories she heard shared one common lesson: "Shun a matrimonial advertisement as you would a serpent!"[156]

NEITHER THE PRESS NOR the police could sort out which of the women coming forward had really married Hoch and which were false leads. Stories were coming in too quickly to be checked. One woman in Peoria even said she was starting a Living Wives of Johann Hoch Association and then turned out not to be one herself.

Often, stories of new victims would be given a lot of coverage before anyone realized they weren't true. Right next to Campbell's January 27 column was a large picture of one Mary Schultz, whom Hoch was said to have lured away from Argos, Indiana, in the summer of 1900. She and her daughter would continue to be listed among Hoch's victims for years (it would have explained his use of the name "Schultz" in 1902), but Hoch had been in jail at the time of their supposed marriage.

Sometimes the story of a possible victim would make news in papers all over the nation, but the announcement that it had been a mistake would be only a tiny item in a local paper, leaving confusion that would linger. Several papers said Hoch had married one Hulda Nagel as "Count Otto Von Kern," but only one tracked Hulda down and talked to her personally (she laughed and said that Mr. Kern had looked nothing like Hoch and had never claimed to be a count). Papers ran large photos of Annie Pratt, who'd been robbed in Ottumwa, Iowa, in 1898, but it all came from a guess made by an Ottumwa photographer. No one talked to Annie herself (or mentioned that she was one of Iowa's most notorious brothel owners). She *had* been married and deserted that year, but the description of the man didn't match Hoch very well.

The timeline and list of victims would soon become a hopeless jumble. But only one murder needed to be proven to get a conviction.

RATHER THAN CONTACT THE Chicago police, Reverend Haass chose to write to Evelyn Campbell, allowing her to break the news that "Hoch" was really Johann Jacob Schmitt of Horrweiler, a fact that had not been in the local papers yet. Minnie Podalski sent Campbell the letters Hoch had written to her in 1903. Johanna Reichel gave Campbell some letters as well.

The police got Campbell an interview with Anna Mary Hendricks, who told her entire story, from her plan to fool the "old codger" who took out the matrimonial ad to the "Dolly Gray" wave.

"I found her to be an unusual type of woman," Campbell wrote. "Refined, intelligent, and sensitive....It is a tragedy to her, this shattering of her happiness and confidence."[157]

She described Hendricks "lifting her fine eyes, heavy with tears," to say, "I was too trusting. My [late] husband, Mr. Hendricks, use to say to me when

An *American* sketch imagining that Hoch had been "inspired" by H.H. Holmes. *From the* Chicago American.

he was alive: 'Mary, you know less of the world than a child,' and I realized it when this man whom I trusted deserted me so cruelly."[158]

One of the people who answered Campbell's plea for clues had been an old neighbor of H.H. Holmes.

"She knew both men in that long ago time," Campbell wrote of her. "She knows enough of that dark page of Chicago's criminal history to keep 'Jacob Schmitt' behind the bars for a long time to come."

The mystery witness claimed that she'd often seen Hoch in the Holmes "castle," experimenting with poisons. Though she didn't remember what name he'd used, she said that she'd known his whereabouts for the last twelve years, but she had kept quiet out of fear. "She knows," Campbell wrote, "that if Jacob Schmitt and the men in his confidence knew she had unsealed her lips, her life would not be worth a farthing."

"How do you know all these things?" Campbell asked her.

"Do not ask me that. I was not the wife of Holmes or even the much-married Schmitt. Perhaps one of them was some kin to me....I could tell you these things if I dared, but I dare not."[159]

Like many reporters, Campbell attempted to use Hoch's birth name, Jacob Schmitt, for a day or so, but soon reverted to calling him Johann Hoch. This was the name that would stick.

In the late nineteenth century, the Swiss scientist Auguste Forel hypnotized an elderly man, handed him a gun, and told him that his assistant was a bad man who should be shot at once. The elderly man pulled the trigger, and the assistant fell.

"He isn't quite dead," said Dr. Forel. "You must fire another shot."

Once again, the elderly man fired without hesitation. He hadn't been told the pistol was loaded with blanks.

Critics brushed it off as theater, with far too many variables uncontrolled, but a growing number of scientists were experimenting with hypnosis by then. Though even Dr. Forel said that cases where it could make people commit crimes were rare, by the turn of the twentieth century, lawyers were claiming their clients had been hypnotized and told to either commit crimes or confess to them more and more. Often, when lawyers or newspapers said a client was "hypnotized," they might as well have been saying they

LAWYER FOR ROESKI

DEMANDS HYPNOTIC TEST TO SAVE BANDIT FROM GALLOWS

EDITION

WOMAN HYPNOTIZES YOUTH INTO PLOT TO WRECK TRAINS

Mrs. Dora Carpenter and Grover Baughman of Tiffin, Ohio, Accomplices in Crime, Are Adjudged Insane.

WOMAN HYPNOTIST.

KILLED AND SEVERAL INJURED BY TRAIN CRASH IN THE UN

CLEWS POINT TO HEITGER IN BEDFORD CASE

All the News of All the World

CHICAGO AMERICAN

Football and Racing News

WEATHER INDICATIONS—GENERALLY FAIR.

VOL. V, NO. 196—P. M. THURSDAY. CHICAGO, NOVEMBER 3, 1904. THURSDAY. PRICE ONE CENT.

BROTHER-IN-LAW SWEARS O'SHEA HYPNOTIZED SLAIN BRIDE

MOTHER SAYS ELOPING GIRL WAS HYPNOTIZED

Emma Kantoos Runs Away With Her Cousin, N. A. Haskins, Taking $3,000 of Her Parent's Money With Her.

COATS AND S

SUNDAY AMERICAN

MESMERIZED INDIANA GIRL SAYS SHE WAS FORCED TO WED

DEFEATS AND FEAR OF DEATH MAKE CZAR A NERVOUS WRECK

INDIANA HEROINE SEEKS HIGH AWARD

Mrs. Kate Hyland of Westport Saves Many Lives.

MRS. CHADWICK'S HYPNOTIC EYE

Six Directors of Wre Bank Subpoenae

Cleveland, O., Dec. 7.—The first mov indictment and arrest of Mrs. Cassie L. Prosecuting Attorney Lee Stroup of Lora b, served subpoenas on the six directors of Bank of Oberlin, O.

President Beckwith, Cashier Spear and the directors are commanded to appear before the grand jury to-morrow to reveal all things they know concerning the affairs

MEMORY LIKE UNTO CAESAR'S

IN GARB OF NUNS THEY TRY TO FREE CONVICTS

Plot to Aid Welland Canal Dynamiters Is Discovered.

IMITATES CAR BARN BANDITS

SAYS SCHWAB IS TRUTHFUL

EASTERN CITY IS FOR HEARST

MONEY DRIVES GHOULS BREAK

Some hypnotism stories from the fall of 1904. *From the* Chicago American.

were coerced or deluded. But other times, hypnosis was held up as a serious process, possibly scientific and possibly supernatural, that could make people do extraordinary things.

That Hoch was a skilled hypnotist was a regular feature in the stories about him. They were probably a comfort to his victims, some of whom felt terribly foolish to have fallen for his cons. If they'd been victims of mind control, how could they be blamed? Maria Julia Doess said that after one meeting with Hoch, she'd been "in his power and did as he wished." She was not herself at all, just a slave to the power of his "hypnotic eye" during their brief marriage.[160]

Evelyn Campbell had recently covered more than one story involving the subject, and in her first interview with Shippy about Hoch, she asked the inspector if he believed Hoch was a hypnotist. He'd chuckled. "A hypnotist of brass and nerve, that's all."[161]

On January 30, the police and press discovered Elizabeth Goerk, Hoch's 1901 wife who had convinced him to study hypnotism. She still had a trunk containing his hypnotism school diploma and the books on the subject she'd convinced him to order, as well as several fake beards and other disguises.

The city reporters must have been absolutely thrilled with such a find and would normally have used it for several headlines across multiple editions. It at least made the front page of the *Journal*'s 5:00 p.m. edition. But it would end up buried by a more important scoop: That evening, Hoch was captured in New York City.

8

CAPTURED

The Chicago police had received a letter from Mrs. August Praxmerer, who'd known Hoch years before, saying that he was in New York. Praxmerer had been avoiding Hoch for years, having heard rumors that he was involved in some sort of diamond theft scheme. But Hoch had managed to pop in on her now and then, including a visit to her Upper East Side home in New York in October 1904, during which he told her he'd be back by Christmas. The holiday had come and gone, but late on January 21, 1905, he appeared again. "He acted very queerly," she wrote. "He was very nervous." He'd sent her son out to buy the Sunday papers, which he seemed to be skimming through for murder stories.[162]

Chief Francis O'Neill of Chicago was confident enough in Praxmerer's lead to contact the New York police to tell them to be on the lookout for Hoch, and he even stated, "We are satisfied he has murdered at least twelve women."[163]

Hoch had, indeed, come to New York, possibly with a stop in Philadelphia (to see if Caroline Streicher had died) on the way. Upon arriving in Manhattan, Hoch checked into his usual New York spot, the Hotel Ridley at 63 Greenwich Street, adjacent to the future site of the World Trade Center. After a few days, he moved to a boardinghouse at 546 West Forty-Seventh Street run by Catherine Kumerle, where he gave his name as Henry Bartels, taking the name of his first Cincinnati wife's previous husband. The place was occupied mainly by German families.

"As you pace down the hall," Evelyn Campbell would later write, "you hear nothing but German conversation and bits of German lieder through thin partitions and from doors ajar."[164]

Mrs. Kumerle belonged to a "widow's club."[165] She had several thousand dollars in the bank and owned a business.[166] To Hoch, she would have seemed like a perfect target. Shortly after renting the furnished room, plus meals, for ten dollars a week, Hoch asked, "Why don't you marry me?"

"I will never marry again unless it's a rich old man," Kumerle said.

"Is your heart cold?" asked Hoch.

"Yes. I have lost faith in you men."

She was peeling potatoes at the time, and Hoch began to help her, noting that he loved potatoes so much he could eat a whole peck of them. Catherine would later confirm that he she had never seen a man eat so many potatoes in her life.

"You puzzle me," she said. "You make me think of stories of Jack the Ripper."

Hoch only laughed.[167]

He told her he was rich, showing her a $700 check and making sure she also saw that he had a large sum of cash in his pocket—probably Emilie's. He asked her what he should do with it. She said he should do what she always did with her money: put it in the bank. He put it in his trunk and said he'd do just that.[168]

And he told Catherine that he knew some of her relatives in Germany. "He did know their names," she later said, "And how that was I can't tell. I never saw such a man. I know about lots of men—I've been married three times—but I never saw such man."[169]

Hoch told her about his last wife, Marie, whom he said had died of blood poisoning in Brooklyn after scratching her hand on a rusty nail.

He continued to propose, promising his landlady that she'd never have to peel another potato if she married him.

"I am tired of being a rolling stone," he told her.

Kumerle protested that she barely knew him, and he said, "Oh, that doesn't make any difference. Marriage is a lottery anyway, and I can show you my record is clear. If you marry me, we can go to Germany, and you can give up this boardinghouse and need never bother about it anymore."[170]

But the act wasn't working. Indeed, comments Kumerle made late in life suggest that she wasn't really interested in men, financially or otherwise. "I think almost any other woman in my position would have listened to him and married him," she said much later, "but I didn't want to be loved. I didn't want a man. I liked to be sociable, but when men made love to me it disgusted me."[171]

And Hoch's attention made her suspicious. "The very thought of marrying such a man was repugnant to me," she said. "Here I am, an old woman, with children grown up and old enough to marry. Why should this stranger make me such a proposal?"[172]

Soon, it would all make sense.

"I remembered reading in the papers about that awful man in Chicago," she said. "And it suddenly flashed across my mind that [this] was the man they call Bluebeard."[173]

She recalled that while telling a story from his life, her boarder had said, "My wife said to me, Jo…or…I meant to say, she called me Henry."[174] And

ELLA WHEELER WILCOX CONTRIBUTES A POWERFUL ARTICLE EACH SUNDAY TO THE GREAT SUNDAY AMERICAN

CHICAGO EVENING AMERICAN

12 O'CLOCK EDITION

WEATHER INDICATIONS—FAIR.

VOL. V., NO. 188—P. 3. TUESDAY. CHICAGO, FEBRUARY 7, 1905. TUESDAY. PRICE ONE CENT.

"HOCK POISONED ME!" CRIES WIFE NO. 44

THIS IS THE WAY JOHANN HOCK TRIED TO HYPNOTIZE MRS KUMMERLE ACCORDING TO HER STORY

Mrs. Amelie Kauke Hock, 14 Douglass avenue, Elgin, who says she married Johann Hock two years ago, making her his forty-fourth wife, has come forward to-day with the accusation: "Hock poisoned me with white powders when I was lying ill."

The woman, who declares she is positive that she married Hock when he posed as a man named Froie, has told the authorities that soon after the mariage she fell ill and was confined to bed. Her husband, she says, attended her and gave her a white powder—the same sort of powder in appearance that has been described in four previous instances in connection with Hock, the police say, and similar to the powder found by the New York police, secreted in a fountain pen owned by Hock when he was arrested.

Immediately after taking the powder, which was administered in a small dose, Mrs. Froie-Hock became much worse.

A physician was hastily summoned when Mrs. Froie became worse and by vigorous action succeeded in saving her. Becoming suspicious of the powder a small portion of it was given to a cat. The cat died within a few minutes, according to Louis Kauke, Mrs. Froie's father.

HER FATHER IDENTIFIES HOCK AS THE MAN.

Kauke, who told the story of his daughter's connection with Froie and of the administration of the powders, has positively identified the picture of Hock as the picture of his daughter's husband, Froie.

Despite the fact that the police say they have sufficient evidence against Hock to have him held for the murder at the coroner's inquest it was decided to-day to postpone the inquiry until the arrival of Hock. Coroner Hoffman announced that the inquest would be again continued for a week to-day. By that time the police will have been able to clinch several minor points in

SEEK GIRL WHO TRIED SUICIDE

Mary Bavisha Prefers Death to Caring for Baby and Attempts End.

NEW WITNESS TO BIG BRIBE IN TUNNEL PLOT

COMERFORD FACES CRISIS IN BRIBE FIGHT TO-DAY

HUGE PETITION BEGS LIFE FOR MRS EDWARDS

How Mrs. Kumerle described Hoch "hypnotizing" her, with an *American* headline that would have used red ink. *From the* Chicago American.

once, she'd found him opening all the bottles of beer in the kitchen, which now seemed strange. Was he thinking of adding arsenic? And she thought of all the times he'd taken her by the wrists and stared into her eyes, making her nervous. Was he trying to hypnotize her? "I began to believe that I had a devil for a boarder," she later said.[175]

While riding the train, she saw someone reading a newspaper with a large picture of the missing "Johann Hoch" and saw that he looked just like her boarder. She bought a copy of the paper when she got to the station to make sure. As Hoch ate dinner, going into his usual routine of all the nice things Kumerle could have if she married him, she set down the paper and said, "I would like to be one of *his* wives. He must have a lot of money to have so many wives!" When she stepped into the kitchen, she looked back to see him tearing the picture from the page, then looking into the mirror, trying to change his appearance.

She persuaded another boarder to "keep him company" and then made her way to the Forty-Seventh Street police station.[176] There, police listened to her story, and a squad of four men, including Officer John O'Neill, was sent to the boardinghouse.[177]

They found Hoch sitting in a rocking chair. He held a book in one hand and smoked a cigar as he chatted with the other boarder.

"Is this Mrs. Kumerle's house?" the officer asked.

"Yes," said Hoch. "But she just went out."

He said that he was not her husband, just a boarder named Henry Bartels. He'd previously lived in Brooklyn, was a salesman for a German wine merchant and had recently kept a saloon on 102nd Street.

When asked to open his trunk, "Bartels" complied, and police dug through it and found, among various items of clothing, a fountain pen and a loaded revolver.[178]

At some point, by most accounts, Officer O'Neill determined they had their man, and he looked at him and said, "Hello, Hoch!"

"How do you do?" Hoch asked. Then he quickly corrected himself and said, "My name's not Hoch, though."

In Hoch's pockets, they found over $600 in cash and change. There were some receipts in his hat from Chicago dated early December 1904. When they showed him the circular Chief O'Neill had sent from Chicago, clearly showing his old mug shot from the Bridewell, Hoch could no longer deny it.

"That's my picture, all right," he said. "But I am a much abused man. I am guilty of no crime and am standing in another man's shoes. They want to make a scapegoat of me, but I can prove my innocence."[179]

Hoch was arrested and taken to the police headquarters downtown on Mulberry Street, where he was photographed, still in his bowler hat, for their famous "Rogues Gallery."

Chief O'Neill told the *Inter-Ocean*, "The wide publicity given to the Hoch case is undoubtedly one of the most potent factors in the rapid and expeditious culmination of the chase."[180]

By the *Chicago American*'s noon edition the next day, it was already running Catherine Kumerle's own story, said to have been dictated by her to one of the Hearst reporters in New York. The quotable Kumerle would prove to be a gold mine for reporters.

"I hated him for his effrontery," Kumerle said. "But there was something about his manner which forbade me telling him. His eyes were trained on mine all the time. I never could forget the way he smiled at me; he seemed to leer like the character in *Faust*—What do you call him?—Mephistopheles."[181]

9

NIGHTS ON MULBERRY STREET

The Mulberry Street police headquarters in New York, with its Rogues Gallery, telegraph room, and detective bureau, was a legend in its own time, connected to every local crime story of the late nineteenth century. But it was on its last legs by January 30, 1905; only three months later, the mayor would lay the cornerstone for the building that would replace it.

In a cell there that night, Johann Hoch—now insisting on that name and denying all others—seemed to invent a new persona for himself. Perhaps he was inspired by the gold statue of Shakespeare's Puck that adorned the headquarters of the humor magazine *Puck*, across the corner from the station. Perhaps he simply thought about what sort of persona could best get him what he wanted, just as he had when courting his wives. In any case, that night, he transformed himself into a charming goofball who seemed like he belonged on a vaudeville stage. None of his wives had spoken of his laugh or his sense of humor before. For the next few weeks, they would be his trademarks.

In the morning, Hoch was walked through Greenwich Village to the Jefferson Market police court to be arraigned. A crowd who'd seen the morning papers followed. "This is a provincial town," he cracked. "I don't blame the Chicago papers for making fun of it. I have had some dealings with the police in Chicago and was never followed by a crowd like this. They wouldn't stand for it."[182]

In the courtroom, he shook his fist at the reporters who'd followed him in and shouted, "Dogs of the press, you are hounding me, and I will get even with all of you!"[183]

Then he calmed down and, perhaps, got into character. Now, he said he was really only wanted for some trouble over his wife's furniture back in Chicago, not bigamy. "Do you think I am a Mormon?" he joked. "Would I be fat and happy if I had twenty-five wives?"[184]

It seemed as though it would take a while to get Hoch extradited to Chicago. "The law requires a legal and bigamous marriage must be proved," said Assistant State's Attorney Newcomer. "Now, who is Hoch's legal wife? That's a puzzler."[185]

One of the best surviving versions of Hoch's New York mug shot. *Author's collection.*

Hoch continued to chat with reporters as he was taken back to Mulberry Street, brushing off the wilder rumors. "Relative to the stories that I once worked for Holmes, the infamous murderer," he said, "they are all false. He was a chemist and I am a machinist. I have read about him and I have seen it printed that I was his janitor. It may have been a man who looked like me, and if his name was Hoch, that's nothing. There are lots of Hochs. I have no fear but that I'll be able to get out of this all right."

Strangely enough, the architect of the Holmes Castle building, Edward Gallauner, had fled Chicago years before and was now living in New York, a short walk from Mrs. Kumerle's. After a knockdown fight with his landlord over the use of foul language, he'd been brought to the same Jefferson Market court only two months before. No one realized it at the time.

Back in his cell, Hoch smoked and talked to anyone who came by, usually joking but sometimes forgetting himself. When presented with a subpar lunch, he became angry and said, "I hope they will take me back to Chicago as soon as possible, where I can have what a white man should."[186]

The police guarding him were impressed by how suave and cool he was. One called him the most remarkable prisoner he'd ever dealt with and said that he had a "facial expression peculiarly persuasive" that made him understand "the magnetic power he had over women."[187]

Even women who hadn't seen Hoch were sending him marriage proposals. He would get a lot of them in the mail in the coming weeks.

Jefferson Market Court, which still stands in New York, where it is now a library. *Library of Congress.*

THE NEWSPAPER WITH THE LARGEST CIRCULATION

ELLA WHEELER WILCOX EACH SUNDAY SUNDAY AMERICAN

CHICAGO AMERICAN

12 O'CLOCK EDITION

CHIEF OF POLICE O'NEILL SAYS TO-DAY--

MORE HOCK WIVES

ARE NOW KNOWN TO US. WE SHALL

PROSECUTE HIM TO THE END

This picture of Hock, reprinted in Hearst's N.Y. Evening Journal, was seen by Mrs. Kimmerle and led to the Bluebeard's arrest.

WOMAN TELLS STORY OF BETRAYING HOCK

RIOTERS STAB SOLDIERS IN POLISH CAPITAL STREETS

CZAR TO SPARE MAXIM GORKY

CHARGES ATTEMPT TO BRIBE GIRL IN SCHAFER MYSTERY

COMPLETE EARLY MARKET NEWS ON THIRD PAGE

CHICAGO AMERICAN

BUSINESS MEN'S EXTRA

HOCK IN COURT

ARRAIGNED ON CHARGE OF

MURDER!

THREE WIVES OF HOCK TO ASK HIS INDICTMENT

"OMAHA" TAKES ANOTHER UPTURN IN WALL STREET

New York, Jan. 31.—Johann Adolph Hock, sought by the Chicago police on suspicion of more than a score of bigamous marriages and half as many mysterious deaths, was hurried to the Jefferson Market Police Court to-day to be arraigned

MERCURY DROP IS PREDICTED

FIGHT TROOPS IN WARSAW WITH FLAMES

HOCK PROMISED MRS. KIMMERLE A HONEYMOON TRIP TO GERMANY

FREES 8-YEAR-OLD SLAYER

4 RUSSIAN DIVISIONS CUT OFF AND ARMY IMPERILED

CHARGES ATTEMPT TO BRIBE GIRL IN SCHAFER MYSTERY

THE NEWSPAPER WITH THE LARGEST CIRCULATION

ELLA WHEELER WILCOX EACH SUNDAY SUNDAY AMERICAN

CHICAGO AMERICAN

AFTERNOON EDITION

HOCK IN JAIL

GUARDED FROM SUICIDE

American's Picture of Hock That Led to His Detection in New York City

BRIBERY IN SCHAFER HEARING

WOMAN TELLS STORY OF BETRAYING HOCK

KEYS TO LEAD TO IDENTITY OF OHIO GIRL MURDERER

New York, Jan. 31.—Watched constantly by special guards at the Tombs to prevent any attempt at suicide, Johann Hock, accused of bigamy and murder,

PHILADELPHIA POLICE HUNT CHARNEL HOUSE

5 O'CLOCK EDITION

CHICAGO AMERICAN

5 O'CLOCK EDITION

"AND THE WAGES OF SIN IS DEATH"

HOCK KILLED 12 WIVES

—Francis W. O'Neill.

GRAFT EXPOSE AT SPRINGFIELD STIRS SOLONS

BIG FOUR AND MICHIGAN CENTRAL PRESIDENTS QUIT

FIGHT TROOPS IN WARSAW WITH FLAMES

FIST FIGHT BREAKS UP SENATE; ARREST EX-SENATOR

HOCK, DECLARING INNOCENCE, REMANDED TO NEW YORK JAIL

4 RUSSIAN DIVISIONS CUT OFF AND ARMY IMPERILED

NIGHT HOME EDITION

CHICAGO AMERICAN

NIGHT HOME EDITION

GRAFT EXPOSED; BOMB EXPLODED IN LEGISLATURE

POLICE DECLARE HOCK KILLED 12 WIVES!

HOCK'S LAST COURTSHIP SHOWS SPEEDY METHODS

Find New Evidence and Declare That Alleged Poisoner Cannot Escape Gallows.

THINKS WIFE'S LOVE IS LOST; KILLS SELF

FIST FIGHT BREAKS UP SENATE; ARREST EX-SENATOR

HOCK, DECLARING INNOCENCE, REMANDED TO NEW YORK JAIL

FIGHT TROOPS IN WARSAW WITH FLAMES

GOLD-FROM-THE-SEA STORY RECALLS GIGANTIC SWINDLE

MERCURY DROP IS PREDICTED

4 RUSSIAN DIVISIONS CUT OFF AND ARMY IMPERILED

INGA HANSON GOES ON

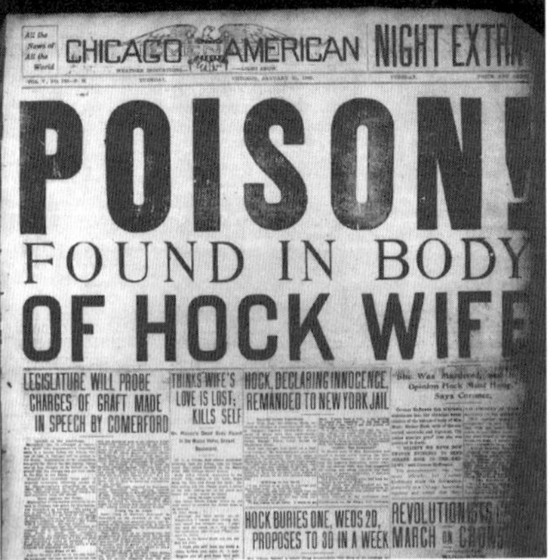
All the News of All the World

CHICAGO AMERICAN

NIGHT EXTRA

POISON!

FOUND IN BODY OF HOCK WIFE

LEGISLATURE WILL PROBE CHARGES OF GRAFT MADE IN SPEECH BY COMERFORD

THINKS WIFE'S LOVE IS LOST; KILLS SELF

HOCK, DECLARING INNOCENCE, REMANDED TO NEW YORK JAIL

She Was Murdered, and Opinion Hock Must Hang, Says Coroner.

HOCK BURIES ONE, WEDS 20, PROPOSES TO 30 IN A WEEK

REVOLUTIONISTS MARCH ON

A montage of *American* front pages from January 31. On the bottom left, the young man pictured is Frank Comerford, who would later play a major role in the story. *From the* Chicago American.

THAT AFTERNOON, EMILIE FISCHER met Elizabeth Goerk in Inspector Shippy's office. They shook hands and congratulated each other on escaping alive, while remarking that they could hardly believe what was happening.

"He was a perfect gentleman," said Fischer, "and I was much surprised by what happened."

"He was such a nice man," Goerk agreed.[188]

That very evening, though, Coroner Hoffman announced that arsenic had been found in the body of Marie Walcker. The *American* rushed out a night extra with "POISON!" in a massive headline over Coroner Hoffman's declaration: "She was murdered, and in my opinion Hoch must hang."[189]

An inquest was scheduled to begin the next morning.

10

THE WIVES AT THE INQUEST

The coroner's jury met at the criminal court building, which stood behind the county jail just above the Loop, mere blocks from where Hoch had lived with Martha Hertzfeld. Several eyewitnesses came, including Anna Hendricks, Emilie Fischer, and Elizabeth Goerk.

When the three wives were first together, Hendricks said, "Well, I never thought it would come to this."

"Yes, I never suspected he was such a man," said Fischer. "He was always good to me and my sister."

"Well, I *always* suspected him," said Goerk. "When he insisted on having my life insured I smelt a mouse. I fooled him, however. He didn't get any of my money. He told me his father had died in Germany and he wanted $500 to go to his old home and get some of the fortune left for him. But I couldn't see it that way. He finally left disgusted and I haven't seen him since. It was good riddance. He was bad rubbish!"

"Well, he was too cute for me," Hendricks admitted. "I gave him $500. All I got in return was a wave of the hand as he left home.…Still, I will say this for him: he was good to me."

"Yes, he was so good and kind to my sister," said Mrs. Fischer. "We were not good friends before he married Mrs. Walcker, but after that he patched the breach between us and we were good friends. After my sister died he felt so lonely and made love to me so ardently that I accepted him and became his wife a week after my sister died."

One of the wives—newspapers didn't say which—said, "Well, he's no good and deserves extreme punishment. I feel sorry for the wife he is said to have poisoned and I only hope they can prove he poisoned her. Then he will be put away for good. He ought to go to the gallows."[190]

Goerk and Hendricks's marriages were proven by witnesses. Two true bills for bigamy were approved by the grand jury, and more meetings were scheduled to look into murder charges.

An hour after the meeting adjourned, Hendricks was in a stateroom aboard the Manhattan Limited train with Evelyn Campbell, bound for New York. Even with the bigamy charge, someone would still have to establish that the man in the New York jail was indeed Hoch. Shippy authorized Campbell to take Hendricks to identify him.[191]

In her column, Campbell wrote of Mrs. Hendricks looking out the window to watch as "the smoky, sooty buildings of the city give way to clean little suburbs, and those again to snow-swept farms." Hendricks said little but spoke in a "mournful cadence…which told me that the humiliated suffering caused by Hock's desertion was still her portion."

"A year ago I was going, a bride, on my honeymoon," Hendricks said. "Mr. Schmitt, when he asked me to go to Germany with him, told me that we would stop in New York and stay a day in the city. And now I am going at a moment's notice to identify him that he may be tried for bigamy, and he is a prisoner awaiting his richly deserved punishment."

By afternoon, the *American*'s headline said that Hoch had murdered sixteen wives.

Inspector Shippy said he was looking into *every* unidentified woman who'd died in the city in the last decade.

"So far," Shippy said, "I have learned enough to convince me the one unidentified victim of the Iroquois fire, and the [one] woman thrown up by the lake at South Haven, were Hoch's wives."[192]

The December 1903 Iroquois Theatre fire had claimed the lives of some six hundred people. Dora Goerk, Elizabeth's grown stepdaughter, had been killed in the blaze. The last unidentified victim's body had lingered at Rolson's Undertaking Parlor before being buried at Montrose Cemetery in June 1904. Exactly what made Shippy think she was a Hoch wife, he didn't say.

Most likely, it was just the sort of thing Shippy *would* say.

11

ANNA HENDRICKS IN NEW YORK

Over the course of the train voyage, Anna Hendricks dictated an article to Campbell, detailing her entire experience. "I know now," she said, "that he must have laughed in his sleeve…to see how easily he was fooling me."[193]

Any fantasies Hendricks may have had of approaching Hoch with a defiant "Dolly Gray" wave were gone. In New York, she and Campbell were brought to the cabinet room on Mulberry Street, where a dozen men were lined up on a stage. Hendricks looked them over.

"It was a drama worthy of the stage," Campbell wrote. "The last time these two had met was in the parlor of Mrs. Hendricks' little cottage in Chicago; then the man had taken his bride of three weeks in his arms and said 'God be with you 'til we meet again.' Now, with the guilt of desertion, thievery, and hypocritical, cruel, lying falsehood between them, the two met again."[194]

"Do you see him?" asked the detective.

"Indeed, I do."

The exact details of what was said next varied from article to article—it was all likely said in German—but the basics were clear. Turning to Hoch, with words that Campbell said held "a world of pain and wounded sensibilities," Hendricks said, "Well, John."

"I'm sorry, Anna," said Hoch.

He began to speak again, apparently to take it back and deny knowing her, but the detective led him and the others away. The identification was complete.

DECLARE POLICE—THREE MORE FOUND TO-DA

HOW WOOING WON HOCK'S ARREST

NEW YORK, Feb. 6.—Mrs. Katherine Kummerle, the German widow who narrowly escaped becoming the last wife of Johann Hock, has related the true story of her adventure with the modern Bluebeard. It was at Mrs. Kummerle's boarding house, 345 West Forty-seventh street, that Hock was taken into custody on information furnished directly by Chief O'Neill of the Chicago police.

"I THINK I'M LUCKY," SAYS WIDOW.

MEETS HER ONE DAY; PROPOSES ON NEXT.

"Well, you are a widow and I am a widower," here he brushed away a tear. "We will get married, no, yes?"

"O, vat a quickness," exclaimed Mrs. Kummerle.

"But I love you, my Katrina, you are my——"

WHERE IS SHE? NEW DOROTHY RUSSELL RUSE

Guesses as to "Hubby" Einstein's Whereabouts Are Also in

MRS. ANNA HENDRICKSON SCHMIDT went to New York at the instance of the Chicago American to identify Hock as her husband. There was a dramatic scene when the two met. "That is the man! That is John!" cried Mrs. Schmidt.

The *American* created a mock-up, mixing photos and drawings of Hendricks identifying Hoch, with Evelyn Campbell looking on. On the right is the trunk Hoch left with Goerk. Newspaper photos of the day were often staged, mocked up, or retouched, and this was by no means a secret. In many cases, it was quite obvious. *From the* Chicago American.

Hendricks later told Campbell that she *wanted* to give him the wave she'd planned before and say, "How do you like 'Goodbye Dolly Gray' now?" but decided that it wouldn't be proper.

On February 3, the *New York Journal*, another Hearst paper, featured a large portrait of Campbell next to its article about the dramatic scene with a caption: "Evelyn Campbell, Who Solved [the] Hoch Case."

LATER, CAMPBELL—AND LIKELY SOME other reporters—approached Hoch in his cell, where he drummed his fingers on the bars.

"Ah, glad to see you," he told her. "I am sorry I have not a better place to receive you. You see, here I lack the—the—"

"The refining influence of a woman?"

"Exactly, exactly. I have been used to it my whole life."

"Then you have been married many times?"

"Only twice."[195]

He laughed and then insisted his only wives where Emilie and Marie.

"But Mrs. Hendricks identified you this morning."

"Oh, her eyesight was always poor." Hoch burst into another long laugh.

"How do you know if she never was married to you?"

"That's the joke!" Hoch said. "Don't ask me to explain now; wait 'til I go to Chicago and then we'll all enjoy the joke, police and all."[196]

Some of his joking threatened to get him in trouble.

"Of what disease did Mrs. Walcker die?" he was asked.

"I ain't no doctor," he said.

"And the others—of what did they die?"

"Oh, some of them died of kidney disease," he began. Then he shook his head, realizing he'd just effectively admitted to several marriages to dead women, and shouted, "I didn't mean that—I didn't hear what you said!"[197]

He said he was disappointed at first that Catherine Kumerle didn't want to marry him but considered himself lucky now that he knew "her true nature." "You don't know what it is to be disappointed in a woman after you get married to her," he said. "Anything is better than that—even jail."

At this, he laughed for some time, until someone told him that Mrs. Kumerle had leaked some important new information to them: something had convinced the police to look inside the fountain pen in his trunk, even though it had to be held under hot water before the barrel would come unscrewed. Inside, there was no pen or ink, just some white powder wrapped in tissue paper. Arsenic.

"It wasn't [my pen]," he said. "I don't know anything about it."

"Well, the police say it contains poison," he was told.

"No, it doesn't," he insisted. "It ain't poison—it's headache powder."

"Oh, then you know something about it!"

Hoch merely laughed again.[198]

Soon, he was back to philosophizing. "My father used to tell me that women would be the ruin of me," he said. "They are always—What you call it?—pulling wool over my eyes. They take advantage of my nature."[199]

Shown a picture of himself with Julia Steinbrecher, his first Chicago wife, Hoch said, "I know the lady, but I can't place the gentleman."

He was given a long list of names of supposed wives. His responses:

> Caroline Hoch, Wheeling: *"Never was there in my life."*
> Mary Warnke Rankin, Chicago: *"Has she got $4000? Would like to meet her when I get back."*
> Martha Hertzfeld, Chicago (now in California): *"Never heard of her. Isn't it ridiculous they have to go way out there and find a wife?"*
> Mary Becher, St. Louis: *"Never married her. She died of kidney trouble, too, I suppose."*

Elizabeth Goerk: *"Who is she?"*
Caroline Streicher, Philadelphia: *"Town too slow for me. Was never there."*[200]

He admitted to marrying Emilie Fischer. "But I don't think it was right for Emilie to go around and help get me indicted just because I was away temporarily," he said. "I intended to come back."[201]

He denied every other name on the list and was largely telling the truth; most of the supposed wives being investigated would turn out to be false leads.

"I suppose I've got to suffer for every man that ever [deserted] a woman," he said. "Come on, ladies, if any of you have lost husbands…just step around and identify me.…Why, I see they now say that an unidentified Iroquois Theatre fire body was that of one of my wives. There's another tip. Ha! Ha! If any lady has disappeared in the last twenty years, just say she was one of Hoch's wives. Oh, this is rich."[202]

Evelyn wrote that he "tittered away to himself in a transport of delight."

"You don't suppose for a minute there's only one man in the country running away from wives?" he shouted. "They are trying to make me stand for all the running away business."

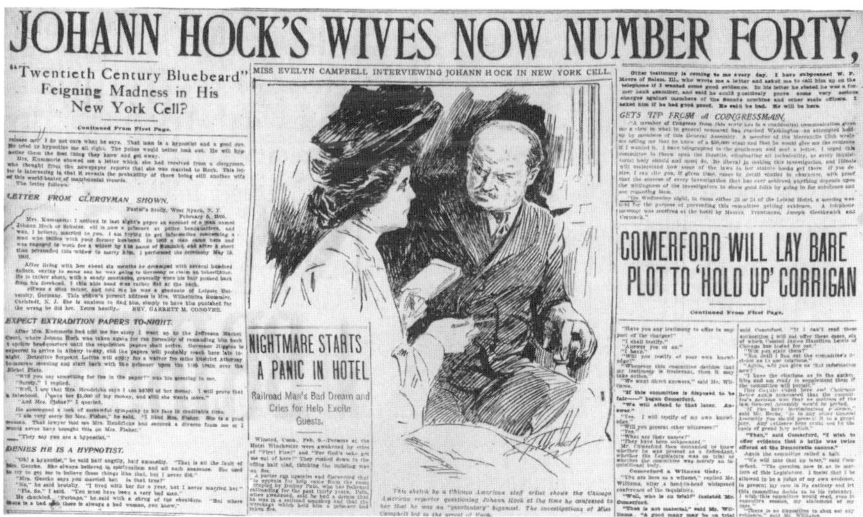

JOHANN HOCK'S WIVES NOW NUMBER FORTY,

"Twentieth Century Bluebeard" Feigning Madness in His New York Cell?

LETTER FROM CLERGYMAN SHOWN.

EXPECT EXTRADITION PAPERS TO-NIGHT.

DENIES HE IS A HYPNOTIST.

MISS EVELYN CAMPBELL INTERVIEWING JOHANN HOCK IN NEW YORK CELL.

This sketch by a Chicago American staff artist shows the Chicago American reporter questioning Johann Hock at the time he confessed to her that he was an "involuntary" bigamist. The investigations of Miss Campbell led to the arrest of Hock.

NIGHTMARE STARTS A PANIC IN HOTEL

Railroad Man's Bad Dream and Cries for Help Excite Guests.

GETS TIP FROM A CONGRESSMAN.

COMERFORD WILL LAY BARE PLOT TO 'HOLD UP' CORRIGAN

A *New York American* sketch of Evelyn Campbell interviewing Hoch in his cell, printed here from the Chicago edition (which also has an article on Frank Comerford). *From the* New York American.

Back in Chicago, Shippy heard reports of Hoch's behavior. "He will laugh on the wrong side of his face when we get him in the sweatbox and put the screws to him," he promised.[203]

THE NEXT DAY, EVELYN Campbell interviewed Hoch as he was walked back through Greenwich Village to the Jefferson Market court. He was handcuffed to Detective Foye but was in good spirits, "as if he was going to a dinner party."

"I tried to hide when I thought the police were after me," Hoch told her. "Any man would do that. But now that they have me, I am ready and anxious to go back to Chicago."

"Do you know there was poison found in the stomach of Mrs. Walcker?"

"Poof," he replied. "Mere doctors' foolishness."

"If you had nothing to conceal, why did you marry Mrs. Hendricks under the assumed name of Jacob Schmitt?"

He glanced sideways. "Who said I used the name of Jacob Schmitt?"

"Why, Mrs. Hendricks, of course."

"Oh, she did? Of course, Mrs. Hendricks is always right. Oh, yes, quite right. Mrs. Hendrick has the certificate, I suppose?"

"Her certificate is in the possession of the grand jury."[204]

"Yes, I suppose I am a bigamist all right," Hoch said. "My first wife, Mrs. Hendricks, came here to identify me, and that fixes that all right, for I guess my other wife, Mrs. Emilie Fischer, is after me in Chicago. It was the fault of a rascally lawyer. He told me Mrs. Hendricks had secured a divorce."

"And are those your only wives?" asked Campbell.

"All but Mrs. Walcker, the one who died in Chicago last September."

"September?" Campbell asked. "I thought her burial record read January 15th of this year."

"Now, I wonder who knows best about that," said Hoch. "The people or I, who was there when that woman died?"

It had, of course, been January.

"Were you a bachelor until you met Mrs. Hendricks in 1903?"

Hoch waved his hand as well as he could while cuffed to a detective. "Sure," he said. "For forty-four years I was a bachelor. I wish."

He paused, and Evelyn suggested, "You wish you were a bachelor still?"

Now, Hoch chuckled.

"Oh, it would hardly be polite to say I wished that," he said. "But I wish I wasn't quite as much married."

He kept up his humorous persona until Campbell chanced to ask about stories that he'd proposed to another woman on his way out of Chicago. Then his angry side appeared.

"They say, they say, they say," he grumbled. "These dogs…why do they not tell the truth? Here are a lot of silly old women running around and saying that I proposed to them and I married them and I deserted them and I killed them. Such monkey work. Who was the woman who said that?"

"Mrs. Johanna Reichel."

"Mrs. Reichel? Why, she is old enough to be my mother."

Campbell noted that she'd like to see the next meeting between Hoch and Reichel after Mrs. Reichel, who was about a decade older than Hoch, heard *that* one. She didn't note that he had called Reichel "dear child" in letters.

"And did you marry Mrs. Steinbrecher or Schultz?"

"Or ninety thousand other women," Hoch said. "No, I didn't marry any of them—that is, not real marriages with certificates and ministers. Why, they have women…who say I was marrying them all the way from 1882. Now, I didn't come to America until 1895, and I certainly didn't send my spirit over here to marry these women. I'm not that crazy about getting married, even if the newspapers and the police do claim that I break the record."

"Won't you tell me just a little something about your life?" Campbell asked.

"What do you want to know?" he asked. "Aren't you scared? You know I propose to everybody. Aren't you afraid I'll propose to you?"

"Not so that anybody could notice it," she said.

"Then maybe *I* ought to be scared. Maybe you are going to propose to me!"

He laughed out loud, then said, "There is one thing I'd like to have straightened out. I hear that I am a chemist, a musician, and have many other occupations. Now, that is all false. I am only a machinist, that's all."

"And you don't play the zither at all?"

Hoch threw his head back and laughed again. "I am sorry to disappoint you, but any woman who says I played the zither to her, or any other kind of a musical instrument, is either telling falsehoods or else has something wrong with her head."

Evelyn confessed in her column that this statement, assuming it was true, disappointed her. "The vision of this pudgy bigamist wooing his wives with the strain of the zither appealed very strongly to me when I heard if from the lips of a friend of one of his wives."

"What do you think about women, anyway?" she asked. "Would you get married again?"

"What?" Hoch asked with another laugh. "Do you want me to have another extra term in prison? I will get out of this scrape first. And I will not say anything against women, either. Women are all right in their place… only one at a time, though."[205]

And with that, Hoch stepped into the Jefferson Market court.

Women crowded around, eager to get a look at the famous lothario. "Well, of all things," said one. "[He] looks like an old clothes man."

"Well, if that's him," said another, "all I've got to say is those widows must have been hard up for husbands."[206]

Back in Chicago, the *Tribune, Chronicle* and *Inter-Ocean* all ran quotes from Evelyn's interviews over the next few days, as did several New York papers and others around the country. Only a few named the woman who was asking the questions. But the *American*'s "Night and Home" edition featured Evelyn Campbell's name in the headline twice, with a picture of her, captioned, "Famous correspondent of the *Chicago American*."

12

THE ORDEAL OF THE BLACK PEN

Hearst's *New York Journal* made a point of quoting Catherine Kumerle as saying she'd seen Hoch's picture in one of *their* papers. So did Pulitzer's *New York World* and at least one German-language paper. The *Journal*, which was probably the one telling the truth, even ran a picture of Kumerle posing with an opened copy of the Sunday paper that contained the photo.

Catherine Kumerle went to speak to Evelyn Campbell at the Mulberry Street police station and put her distinct flair for the dramatic on full display.

"The police warned me to say nothing to anybody, especially newspaper reporters," she told her. "But I think this is a thing that people should know."

Evelyn was happy to talk and asked her about the arsenic reportedly found in Hoch's room. Mrs. Kumerle said the police showed her a "syringe" that contained arsenic, and Evelyn had soon arranged for a photograph of it to be taken.

"I have read of the evidence you collected," Kumerle told Evelyn. "And I wanted you to know what I know about him....I was afraid of him from the first. He was too plausible, too good....I said to myself, 'There is something wrong. Rich men do not carry their own trunks.'"[207]

Once, when Kumerle left the boardinghouse, Hoch had asked her if she was going to the bank.

"I wished to say no," she said. "But his eyes were on mine, and I could only admit weakly that I was. Then he took me by the wrists as he had done several times, rubbing them slightly with his thumbs, and asked if he could

SHE CAUGHT HIM BY

king Described by Mrs. Kum-
ever Recognition of Man
Wives, Led to Arrest.

MRS. KUMMERLE IDENTIFYING HOCK
FROM AN EVENING JOURNAL PICTURE

'S WIVES; COUNT 'EM.

TELLS HOW "BLUEBEARD"
WON HEART AND HAND

JOHANN HOCK'S PHOTO, TAKEN BY THE POLICE

The *New York Journal*'s mock-up of Kumerle reading their paper, as well as a murky version of Hoch's New York mug shot. *From the* New York Journal.

go with me. Fear possessed me, and I wrenched my arms away and left him.…Whenever he took hold of my arms and looked into my eyes I could not help answering his questions.…He is a hypnotist, and a good one, and he tried to hypnotize me."[208]

A *New York Herald* reporter went to see Catherine at the boardinghouse and was amused by her confusing the words "Bluebeard" and "Bluebird." To him, she lamented the financial loss the case had brought her, first by Hoch's voracious appetite, then by his not paying her back a dollar she'd paid to have his laundry done, and then by the loss of business. The police didn't want her renting Hoch's former room to anyone else until the investigation was over.

She pointed to a chiffonier and said, "It was in there they found the fountain pen with the powder in it….The detective told me he thought it was poison. Now they're mad because I've told it, but I don't see why I shouldn't. I've had enough trouble with these policemen coming here all the time and I can't rent my room for $3 a week, which I ought to have. Why shouldn't I tell what I found? They won't pay me if I don't tell."

"You know he says he doesn't play or know anything about music?" she asked. "Well, the first thing he asked about after he came in here was a piano. He wanted to know if I wouldn't get him a piano. Now, what did he want that for?"

She mentioned that he'd given her a gold ring with a blue stone, which she'd taken without agreeing to marry him. "Well, it's a good thing I didn't," she said with a laugh. "I've had three husbands and I can get another if I want to, but I never expect to see a man that can look into your eyes or say such words as this 'Bluebird.'"[209]

FORTY-EIGHT HOURS AFTER HOCH'S first trip to the court, his extradition papers had still not arrived, so Hoch was taken again for paperwork to be formally held in the Mulberry Street station another night. He saw Evelyn Campbell there and called her over.

"Will you say something in the paper for me?" he asked.

"Surely."

"Well, I see that Mrs. Hendricks says I took $500 of her money. I will prove that a falsehood. I gave her $1,000 of *my* money, and still she wants more."

"And Mrs. Fischer?" Campbell asked. She noted that it took him a moment to affect a look of remorse, but he managed it.

"I am very sorry for Mrs. Fischer," he told her. "I liked Mrs. Fischer. She is a good woman. That lawyer told me Mrs. Hendricks had secured a divorce or I never would have brought this on Mrs. Fischer."

Taking advantage of the prisoner's attention, Campbell said, "They say you are a hypnotist."

"Oh, a hypnotist!" he replied in a tone Campbell said was halfway between amusement and anger. "That is all the fault of Mrs. Goerk. She always believed in spiritualism and all such nonsense. She used to try to get me to believe those things like that, but I never did."

"Mrs. Goerk says you married her," says Evelyn. "Is that true?"

"No," he said. "I lived with her for a year, but I never married her."

"Fie, fie," Evelyn scolded. "You must have been a very bad man."

Hoch laughed again and shrugged his shoulders. "Perhaps. But where there is a bad man there is always a bad woman, you know."[210]

A *New York American* reporter interviewed Reverend Haass at his new office in Utica. He still believed that Hoch had survived the wreck of the *Elbe*.[211]

The *New York Journal* said that Hoch told Detective Foy six tips for winning a woman:

1. Nine out of every ten women can be won by flattery.
2. Never let a woman know her shortcomings.
3. Always appear to a woman to be the anxious one.
4. Women like to be told pleasant things about themselves.
5. When you make love, be ardent and earnest.
6. The average man can fool the average woman if he will only let her have her own way at the start.[212]

"Make love" in this context meant "flirt"; Hoch never referred to physical activity. Later, he would be quoted as saying, "I did not love any of my wives. I have no use for women. It was purely a business proposition with me.… Flattery was my chief stock in trade. You can win a woman quicker that way than any other."[213]

13

THE ROAD TO CHICAGO

On the morning of February 8, Hoch was taken to Jefferson Market court for the last time. An official asked his name, and Hoch said, "Johann Hoch. H-O-C-H. And you pronounce it just like you do when you 'hoch der kaiser.'"

He was given a form to sign, and then he turned to Detective Loftus of Chicago and said, "Now I am your prisoner."[214]

The journey to Chicago began with a walk to the Hudson. As they strolled, a crowd formed.

"Ain't I a dandy?" Hoch said. "I'm famous, what? I'm a first-class, high-toned gentleman, and I ain't no loafer!"[215] When the crowd laughed at his accent, which the *New York Mail* said suggested "a knockabout German comedian,"[216] he shouted, "Never mind. You are all loafers!"[217]

He tried to dodge photographers, but when they cornered him with cameras, he held up his hands and joked, "Don't shoot, I surrender!"[218] When a flashbulb went off, he visibly jumped and said, "I have such a nervous with them things. Don't do it again."[219]

Loftus escorted Hoch to the Barclay Street Ferry,[220] which took them across the Hudson to the Lackawanna railroad station in Hoboken. As Hoch boarded the train, another group of women crowded against the car to get a look at him. They were reportedly satisfied when he stuck his head out the window to call them "rubbernecks." He laughed and shouted, "Ha! I scare you! Ha!"[221]

ELLA WHEELER WILCOX CONTRIBUTES A POWERFUL ARTICLE EACH SUNDAY TO THE GREAT SUNDAY AMERICAN

CHICAGO AMERICAN

AFTERNOON EDITION

WEATHER INDICATIONS—SNOW FLURRIES.

VOL. V., NO. 190—P. M. THURSDAY. CHICAGO, FEBRUARY 9, 1905. THURSDAY. PRICE ONE CENT.

"I HAVE EVIDENCE TO HANG HOCK"

This is Hock guarded by detectives speeding today to Chicago to face accusers.

COMERFORD IN NEW FIGHT TO EXPOSE GRAFT

NEW RELIGION FINDS VICTIM

Utica, N. Y., Pastor Coming He to Prove "Bluebeard" Guilty.

While the train bearing Johann Hock, bigam and alleged wife poisoner, is speeding on its way Chicago to-day, the Rev. Sherman C. A. Haas, past of St. Matthew's German Lutheran Church of Ut

The *American* pasted the New York mug shot onto a drawing to portray Hoch on the train with Loftus. Another Comerford article is visible. *From the* Chicago American.

"Probably you could win some of those nice-looking women outside even now," Loftus told him.

"Oh, I suppose I am through with women for a while."[222]

Evelyn Campbell, while boarding the train with him, spotted his game at once: "His chief concern," she wrote, "appeared to be procuring the good opinion of Detective Sergeant Michael Loftus. He seems to care more for that than for the denying of the various charges brought against him."

"I do not wish to make you the slightest trouble," Hoch told the detective. "I want to prove to you that I, too, can be a gentleman."[223]

Turning to Campbell, he said "I have no quarrel with the police. Indeed, I gave myself up to them. It was I who told Mrs. Kumerle to tell the police….I gave her $10 and she did as I requested."

Campbell exchanged glances with Loftus. Hoch's charm offensive wasn't working on her. "I have never seen a prisoner more insatiably vain,"[224] she wrote, "or keener for attention, no matter of what sort, than Johann Hoch."

A *New York World* reporter said he could understand how Hoch's "poor dupes" would fall for him but noted, "Looking him over, one wouldn't lend him a good horse."

Hoch forgot his new humorous persona now and then and let his anger take over. After claiming to have surrendered himself, he ranted that Mrs. Kumerle was lying about being hypnotized and about his proposal. He even accused her of stealing diamonds that he'd kept in the room.[225]

Loftus, too, alternated between joking with Hoch and needling him. He warned him that fourteen wives would be lined up to meet him when they arrived. Hoch brushed it off and said it would be just like when a woman came to identify him in his cell days before, "But she did not know Johann Hoch from the man in the moon."[226]

When the train left the city and Hoch tried to lower the curtain on his window, Loftus told him, "Put it up. You'll never see this country again."[227]

FRANCES MAULE, A REPORTER for the *New York American*, rode on the train from Hoboken to Dover, New Jersey.

"It seemed impossible to take seriously this humorous German," she wrote, "with his sharp little blue eyes and cynically laughing mouth. He certainly did not take himself seriously. He laughed at everything and when there was nothing to laugh at he made new jokes to keep the ball rolling. The trip to Dover was more like a gay excursion than the start toward retribution of a man accused of an ever-growing number of hateful crimes."[228]

"Are you sorry to leave New York?" Maule asked him.

"Oh, yes," Hoch said. "The newspapers have made it pleasant for me. But then just think how glad I will be to get back to Chicago—and to all my dear wives!"[229]

Maule, a former *Chicago American* reporter, would go on to be one of the most famous openly lesbian writers of her time. She didn't find Hoch magnetic at all. "But," she wrote, "in a low comedy way, he is what is popularly known as 'good company,' an amusing, mildly cynical sort of fellow, with a vital and virile flow of spirits. One could imagine such a man bringing into the dull, drab existence of the ordinary, rent-haunted haus frau of the German districts in Chicago a glimpse of the brighter and merrier life." She was unaware that none of his previous wives had described him as such a joker.[230]

An illustration in the *New York American* (seen on page 9 of this book) shows Maule with Evelyn Campbell in the car, asking questions while Hoch and the men around him laugh. Campbell herself had noted that she felt very "green" when she tried to trip Hoch up with documents and data, only to be brushed off. But when Maule asked Hoch about his hypnotism degree, she seemed to have better luck.

"That was nothing," Hoch said. "I did that to oblige my wife. One day she reads it in the paper an advertisement that you should become a spiritualist and a hypnotist for $5, and she says to me, 'Johann, we should send for that.' I said there is nothing in it, but she wanted to be what you call a medium, so I send to the professor in Jackson, Michigan, and get a little book which shows how you make it with your hands to become a hypnotist, and my wife she takes it and studies it and pretty soon she puts a sign in the window saying that she is a spirit medium."

"What was her name?"

"Goerk, I think."

"But I thought you said you had married only two women."

"Well, you see, some people might call it being married to Mrs. Goerk, and some of them mightn't."[231]

Professor Harradan's hypnosis book advised holding a bright object in front of a subject and saying, "You are getting sleepy…very sleepy." Once a hypnotized subject was in a trance, it said, one could make them believe they were a dog, a pig, or Socrates. If that wasn't amusing enough, you could make them think a bowl of flour was ice cream and eat it was delight. Had it included the line "Make sure your subject is willing to play along," it would have been an excellent guide to staging a comedy hypnosis show.

"I didn't study it," Hoch explained. "You can get [the diplomas] by the bushel for five dollars apiece."[232]

In Buffalo, the party switched from the Lackawanna Railroad to the Nickel Plate Road. There, a reporter asked Hoch about the news that arsenic had been found in Marie Walcker's body.

"Don't chew the rag about that," said Hoch. "Don't talk foolishness."

"This isn't foolishness; this is something exceedingly serious for you."

"Arsenic? Pooh. It was her kidneys that killed her."

When asked about the arsenic in the fountain pen, Hoch said, "That's more foolishness. If you want to find out that is tooth powder. Now, you see you are not so smart, eh?"

"Don't you think a fountain pen holder a strange place to keep tooth powder?" he was asked.

"I am not thinking about strange things. That is the newspapers' business, not the sheet metal business. I am a man who sticks to his trade."[233]

Campbell noted that Hoch contradicted himself so frequently that it was impossible to know when to believe him. In telling his life story to a *New York World* reporter, he gave the correct name of the ship he'd sailed on in 1895, though he insisted he hadn't left a wife or any children in Germany.[234]

When someone mentioned Horrweiler, Hoch claimed he had never heard of the place. Loftus showed Hoch a photograph of himself as a younger man, with a caption on the back naming him Jacob Schmitt of Horrweiler—it was the very photograph that Reverend Haass had mailed to Chicago years before.

"Well, that's my picture," Hoch admitted. "I guess it is, but how did that get [to Chicago from] Europe?"

"The minister who says he married you in Wheeling sent it over there," said Loftus.

Hoch flinched visibly and then regained his composure and laughed. "There it is again, more foolishness."[235]

Campbell continued to try to trip him. When he said he married Anna Hendricks in 1900, she said, "But Mr. Hoch, Mrs. Hendricks's first husband was alive and living with her in 1900."

"So?" he asked. "Well, maybe her husband was living when I married her. I don't know."[236]

At one point, he insisted Anna Hendricks had been his first wife. "I married [her] and we had a fight—you know how the Dutch fight—and then it was all over....I heard she got a divorce a couple of years ago....If I have put my foot in it, and she is still my wife...why, I'll say 'guilty' and take a year [in jail for bigamy] and call myself night and morning a damn fool."[237]

A *New York World* article filed from the Binghampton station noted, "Johann Hoch is no man's fool. He said that more than once today in a vainglorious way, but he is pleased to have one take him for a woman's fool."[238]

At Bellevue, Ohio, Hoch moved to the window to blow kisses to the crowd. In Cleveland, Evelyn Campbell noted that Hoch was disappointed that no crowd had gathered to see him. "Where is my reception?" he asked. "I do not see any people on this platform. That is a shame. I want my due."

Sometimes, reporters would tell him the latest developments, such as the news that Amelia Kauke of Elgin, Illinois, had named Hoch as the man who married and deserted her in 1902 (a claim that would never be confirmed). Turning to Evelyn at one point, he asked, "Will you do something for me, Miss Campbell?"

"Certainly, if I can."

"I want you to get those people who accuse me to face me."

"Why, I did my level best," she said. "I brought Mrs. Hendricks."

"Poof," he said, with a wave of his hand. "I want you to bring that woman from Elgin who said I tried to poison her and that man [in Argos] who is hunting his sister and all the rest of them. I want to see them all. I am no coward."[239]

The trip normally took around twenty-four hours, but the snowy conditions slowed the train down.

Several reporters came aboard at Fort Wayne, Indiana. Hoch greeted them holding a pink carnation.

"You don't look like a man who has anything to worry about," one said.

"Why should I?" he asked. "I'm feeling splendid."[240]

A *Chicago Evening Journal* reporter among the new crowd told Hoch that he was likely to be shown a photograph of Marie Walcker's body, taken in her coffin when it was exhumed.

"Do you think I am afraid of her?" he asked. "She's dead, ain't she? Why should I be afraid of dead folks? Dead women can't hurt me. Live ones can. I would rather face a lot of dead ones than all the women who think they are married to me. No man has ever been hurt by a dead person, I guess. I don't believe in ghosts." He looked out the window a moment and then said, "I guess she'll stay dead."[241]

Campbell noted that toward the end of the trip, Hoch finally seemed to be getting nervous. He was visibly disturbed when a group of schoolchildren at the station in Knox, Indiana, shouted, "Get a rope! String him up!"

When another gaggle of reporters got onto the train, Hoch and Loftus disappeared into an empty part of the train and stayed there for the rest of the trip to Chicago.[242]

At one point a reporter heard Campbell ask for a statement and said Hoch's reply was "grossly insulting, and more so as it was given through the smile which seems to be a part of his cunning makeup."[243] More than one paper reported that he'd said something particularly vile to her. She apparently took it in stride. What else could she do?

The *New York Herald* referred to Evelyn Campbell as a "special commissioner" on the case. Several papers showed illustrations of her talking with Hoch, and a photograph of her was on the front page of an Evansville, Indiana paper that credited her, personally, with getting Hoch captured and charged. These weren't even Hearst papers. The Hoch story had brought her acclaim from all quarters.

14

BACK IN TOWN

While the train crept through the snow, the coroner's inquest resumed in the Chicago Avenue police station. On its second day, the meeting consisted of only Bertha Sohn talking about Marie Walcker's courtship, marriage, and death.

By the time it ended, a crowd, estimated to be between two and three thousand strong, had jammed the LaSalle Street station, waiting for Hoch to arrive. "It was a motley array," wrote the *Tribune*. "Craning their necks at every sound of a bell, they would cry 'Hoch's coming!' only to be disappointed when they found it was merely an empty suburban train backing into the station."[244]

When Hoch did arrive, he rubbed his eyes and looked out into the trainyard. He couldn't see the crowd from where he was, just a couple of other trains and a handful of guards and ushers.

"Where are those fourteen wives you talked so much about?" he asked.

"Maybe they missed their cars," Loftus joked.

"I think you have been joshing me about that part of the business," Hoch said. "There couldn't be fourteen wives, anyway, for I never had that many."[245]

Loftus hustled him into a service elevator to the street level, where a patrol wagon was waiting. Before they drove away, though, the assembled "rubbernecks" had gotten word of the ruse and crowded around the wagon.

"No president of the United States ever had a greater reception than I am getting," Hoch beamed. "Were any of those forty-four wives you talk about in that motley crowd?"

NIGHT AND HOME EDITION

CHICAGO EVENING AMERICAN

WEATHER INDICATIONS—FAIR AND COLD.

VOL. V., NO. 191—P. M. FRIDAY. CHICAGO, FEBRUARY 10, 1905.

ARCH-BIGAMIST HOCH READY FOR THE INQUEST IN CRIMINAL COURT BUILDING.

From a photograph posed especially for a Chicago American staff artist.

The much-married man, well groomed and self-possessed, is shown ready to face ordeal with the inquisitors. Reading from left to right, the picture shows Inspector Shippy, Detective Michael Loftus, who brought the prisoner from New York; JOHANN HOCH and Coroner Hoffman.

300 SHOT IN ST. PETERSBURG IN RIOTS IN POLAND; 12,000 STRIKE

Special to the American.

St. Petersburg, Feb. 10.—New and stupendous strikes and bloody street battles of the last few hours indicate that the situation in Rus-

ALDERMEN TO BE ON RACK IN TUNNEL DEAL

CHILD BURNED TO DEATH

TWO OTHERS HURT IN FIRE

One child was burned to death and two others severely injured in a fire at 68 Oak street to-day.

The dead:

MARGARET SANGHLEVOGLIO, five years old.

Inspector George Shippy, Detective Michael Loftus, Johann Hoch, and Coroner Peter Hoffman at the Chicago Avenue Police Station upon Hoch's arrival. *From the* Chicago American.

"I guess they were all there," said Loftus. "And you owe me a good cigar for sneaking you away from them!"[246]

Hoch smiled at the yelling crowd as he was driven to the East Chicago Avenue police station and hustled inside. With three stories and a tower, the station looked like a smaller, "second city" version of the castellated Jefferson Market court in New York. No one mentioned it, but in July 1903, Marie Walcker had had her previous husband, Emil, arrested at the same station after the last time he struck her and threatened to kill her. He was fined twenty-five dollars.

Once uncuffed from Loftus, Hoch threw off his overcoat and sat in an armchair, facing another gaggle of reporters.

"I have absolutely nothing to say," he told them. "Go away from me, you fellows. If all you told about me was true, hanging is too good for me, but it is all a pack of lies. A pack of lies, I tell you!"

"But we want to tell your story, tell what you have to say," said a reporter.

"I've got nothing to say at all. All you can do for me is convict me. You and the police, I suppose, will make a good job of it."[247]

He was right to be worried about the press and police's impact on his case; he would have had an uphill battle even if he *had* been innocent. The job of the police was to get convictions, not necessarily the truth. Chief O'Neill, Coroner Peter Hoffman, and Inspector Shippy all already said publicly that they could prove Hoch was a murderer. Anything other than a conviction would be humiliating to them by now, no matter what the investigation showed. O'Neill would survive his term without major accusations of corruption (he would eventually be better known for his efforts to preserve Irish folk music than his police work), but Shippy and Hoffman were another story. A former railroad clerk and county commissioner, Hoffman had no training in medicine or forensics; most of that work was left to the various coroner's physicians, who acted under his orders. He was only a month into the job now, but stories of him and Inspector Shippy pulling dirty tricks to get convictions would one day be legend. If Shippy and Hoffman failed to find evidence against Hoch, they'd probably plant some. If they found evidence exonerating him, they'd likely suppress it.

Hoch was brought into Shippy's office to meet the people who'd come to identify him. He smiled and twiddled his thumbs while he waited[248] and then jumped up when Dr. Reese arrived. He grabbed his hand and said, "Hello, Doc! You are looking fine, too. Chicago agrees with you, yes?"[249]

Benno Lechner, who'd been the best man at Hoch's first Chicago wedding nearly a decade before, came in and was recognized immediately.

"Well, Benno!" said Hoch. "You are certainly looking fine![250] Come and see me again. I'll be in the jail every afternoon for a while, they tell me."[251]

In the hall, Lechner told reporters, "Say, but that man is the limit. I stood up with him when he married Mrs. (Julia) Steinbrecher, who was a relative of mine, and I furnished a wine supper afterward. He still owes me $200 for that dinner. And say—he sits there as cool as a cucumber, and no matter what they say to him it doesn't faze him a bit. I wish I had that $200!"[252]

The first wife to be brought in was Minnie Warnke, who had finally admitted to marrying Hoch. Days before, the police had spoken with Herman Domke, her ex-husband, and then brought her in for another round of questioning. She broke down after Gustav Strelow and Justice Kaufman were brought before her, wedding paperwork in hand. She and Strelow accused each other of various murders and other crimes, but the police hadn't cared about other charges. The important thing was connecting her to Hoch in time for his arrival.

Now, brought before Hoch with her collar pulled high enough to hit the brim of her green feathered hat, Minnie pointed Hoch out at once. "I see him, that's him!" she shouted. Then, after staring at him for a few seconds, she reared back, as though about to pounce, and said, "But did you didn't get none of my money!"[253]

"Be careful," Hoch said. "You know you are a bigamist as well as I."

She quieted down quickly.

Next was Elizabeth Goerk, who hesitated a little at the door. She'd told the *Daily News* she never wanted to see Hoch again and didn't care what happened to him.[254] Shippy took her by the arm. "If you find your husband in here he will probably be tickled to death to see you," he said.[255]

She stepped into the room and looked at everyone else present before her eyes landed on Hoch. A reporter said her face displayed a mix of shock and anger.

"That is my husband, Inspector," she whispered. "Yes, that is the man I married."[256]

"Well, you have told a pack of lies about me!" said Hoch. "You called me a hypnotist and said I was trying to get your money when you know I was a good husband to you."[257]

Goerk's fear fell away, and she snapped back at him. "Now, John, you know you did not treat me right," she said. "You know you deserted me."

Hoch grinned. "Perhaps you made life miserable for me. Perhaps I couldn't stand to live with you."[258]

Goerk was taken back out, where reporters were awaiting her reaction. "Oh, he recognized me all right," she said. "He looks better than he did when I saw him last. But he said I lied to the police about that hypnotism business and other things. Then he laughed and joked about me!"

"Do you think he ever loved you?" a reporter asked.

"That man love a woman?" she sneered, stamping her foot for emphasis. "Hoch never loved a woman in his life. Women to him are like poison to his tongue. All he wants is their money and their property…but I fooled him!"[259]

Ellen Hoppe, who'd only just told the police she was one of Hoch's victims, came in next, and Hoch grinned broadly.

"Not guilty this time, inspector," he said. Turning to Ellen, he said, "How do you do my good lady?"

Ellen admitted that she had the wrong man.

"But if you don't get her away from me, by George, I will marry her, Inspector!"[260]

Fred Magerstadt, the furniture dealer who'd had Hoch arrested years before, was brought in.

"Did you ever prosecute this man?" asked Shippy.

"Yes, I did once," said Fred.

"Twice, you mean, my dear sir," Hoch corrected. He then corrected Magerstadt a bit on the stories he'd been telling, particularly the detail about selling Hoch furniture in 1891 and 1892. Magerstadt had, in fact, probably been off by several years.

"You are right, Hoch," Magerstadt said. "You have got it all down pat."[261]

"You bet your life," said Hoch.[262]

Shippy asked Hoch about the story of him leaving clothes on the banks of the Ohio River, and Hoch simply grinned.

The last of the wives was Emilie Fischer, who came in shouting that Hoch was a "dirty dog."

"You married my sister and killed her!" she shouted in German. "Then you married me; you are the man and you took my $750 and left me like a dog. You are a villain and a cur."

"You are telling a pack of lies," said Hoch. "You know your sister was sick and died. I am so sick of this business."[263]

When the witnesses were dealt with, it was time for the officials to begin the process of "sweating," a process that often involved beatings, mind games and torture in order to get a confession. This case was too closely watched for them to get away with their more extreme methods. State's attorney Olson asked most of the questions, though Shippy, Loftus and, occasionally, Mrs. Fischer, who was in the room part of the time, would break in. Hoch repeated his basic stories of Marie's death and said that he had put arsenic in the fountain pen to kill himself, though he insisted on telling that portion to Olson and Loftus privately, where Emilie couldn't hear.[264] Little effort was made to trick him into a confession that night; they simply let Hoch make his statements. A transcript would be read at the trial.

Around 2:00 a.m., Hoch was led to a bed and allowed some sleep. The *Inter-Ocean* noted, "He appears well fed, good humored, and not at all anxious as to what is to befall him."[265]

15

THE INQUEST CONTINUES

The next morning was bitterly cold, and Hoch seemed groggy when he was taken to the criminal court building for the inquest. He was seated at the head of the witness table, near Hoffman, Shippy, and Loftus. Other witnesses, including Emilie, sat around the table. A jury sat in chairs along the wall.

With Hoch was Isadore Plotke, whom he had engaged as his lawyer. Plotke would later be described as having "a Charlie Chaplin–like personality and a Weber and Fields (slapstick German) dialect." He stood five feet, four inches tall[266] and looked at least a foot shorter in photographs—indeed, he looked like the sort of diminutive man who would be the laughingstock of the office in a *Twilight Zone* episode. He said little at the inquest and impressed no one.

Though no one seemed to realize it at the time, Plotke had been Marie Walcker's lawyer in her 1903 divorce. Perhaps Hoch or Plotke thought it would make Hoch's case more compelling if his supposed victim's own lawyer was on his side, but it also could have been seen as a conflict of interest. It can't have been a coincidence in a city crawling with lawyers. But so far as is known, neither ever spoke of Plotke's connection to Marie, and it never came up.

Hoch looked tired at the inquest. He kept his overcoat on and drummed his fingers against the table and chair. The *Journal* wrote that he resembled "a low-class German or Jewish immigrant—the kind of face you see bending over the coats and trousers in the sweatshop rooms, and, later, see directing these same sweatshops with [an] unfeeling, hawk-eyed gaze."[267] The *Chicago*

COMERFORD WILLING TO RUN ONCE MORE

Exiled Lawmaker Will Be Candidate in Second District if Governor Deneen Orders a Special Election to Fill the Vacancy.

CONFIDENT VOTERS WOULD VINDICATE HIM AS MARTYR

County Clerk Olsen Awaits Orders From Springfield Requesting Election of New Legislator—House Might Reject if Elected.

Frank D. Comerford will be a candidate for re-election as Representative from the Second senatorial district, if Governor Deneen orders an election to fill the vacancy made by the expulsion of Mr. Comerford.

"If the people of my district think I did right in attempting to expose the boodlers in the Legislature and ask me to be a candidate I shall make the race," he said. "The people will have an opportunity to give a stinging rebuke to my detractors. It's up to them to say what shall be done."

Mr. Comerford's friends are at work for him, and will endeavor to secure him the nomination. It is said there is considerable sentiment in the district favoring his return to Springfield.

Might Be Barred if Elected.

Whether he would be given his seat, if elected, is another question. The Legislature has the power to pass on the qualifications of its members, and it may decide that a member once expelled is not qualified to sit in the House.

Olsen Awaits Notice.

Governor Deneen has not yet notified County Clerk Olsen of the vacancy existing in the Second senatorial district. The state constitution declares that when a vacancy occurs in either house, the Governor, or persons exercising the powers of Governor, shall issue a writ of election to fill such vacancy. The Governor can direct the county clerk to call a special election to fill the vacancy, but until the chief executive of the state takes such action, the county clerk can make no move.

Comerford Shuts Up.

Mr. Comerford said he had decided to stop talking about his case. He is busy preparing evidence to be submitted to the grand jury. He said he was satisfied he could obtain the indictment of two or three of the boodlers and send them to the penitentiary. He declined to discuss his plans, as that would put on their guard the men he is after.

"I made good on the attempt to bribe Lurton and my charges against Mitchell, but the committee was against me," he said. "It was Mitchell's word against mine. Before a jury the weight of the evidence would have been in my favor, because Mitchell had a motive in not telling the truth."

Socialists See Party Peril.

The Socialists are taking an interest in the case of Mr. Comerford. They say if the power of the Legislature is as broad as that exercised against the Representative from the Second district its members may expel any one who may entertain views differing from theirs.

Former Official Indicted.

PORTLAND, Ore., Feb. 10.—Ex-United States Attorney John Hall was indicted today by the federal grand jury in connection with the land frauds cases under course of investigation.

American Is Convicted.

CINCINNATI, Ohio, Feb. 10.—Councilman Joseph Schweninger, indicted for permitting gambling in his place of business, pleaded guilty today and was fined $100 and costs.

ARREST ACCUSED SENATOR.

Fourth California Legislator Now Under Bail Bonds.

SACRAMENTO, Cal., Feb. 10.—Senator Eli Wright, indicted by the grand jury of Sacramento county last night on a charge of bribery, was arrested today. He was held in custody for some time while his attorneys could hunt for bondsmen, which they finally found.

Senators Bunkers, French, and Emmons, also indicted for bribery, who were placed under arrest last night, have been released on bail of $5,000 cash. Under the rules of the Superior court of this county, the accused Senators will be arraigned on Saturday, Feb. 18.

BIGAMIST'S CHARACTERISTIC EXPRESSION AT INQUEST, THREE OF HIS ODD POSES, CORONER, AND LAST MRS. HOCH.

HOCK UNMOVED BY CHARGES OF WIFE

Leers Complacently at Former Mrs. Fischer, While She Relates Story of Sister's Death and Courting Beside of Corpse.

(Continued from First Page.)

stairs and found her apparently asleep from sheer exhaustion.

"She was lying on her side. I thought I had better let her sleep, as she had had trouble and suffered agony for almost four weeks, and had none or little sleep."

Above: Scenes from the inquest as reported in the *Daily Inter-Ocean. From the* Daily Inter-Ocean.

Opposite: The hapless lawyer Isadore Plotke. *From the* Chicago Daily News.

Sun, too, noted "He is Jewish looking....He might be taken for a prosperous Halsted street merchant."[268]

At times, Hoch even nodded off, but he woke up when Emilie Fischer took the stand. "Both of my sisters seemed jealous because I had accumulated a little money," she said. "We made up that evening and agreed to let bygones be bygones. My sister introduced me to Hoch as her husband and I said that I was very glad to meet him."

"Are you glad now that you have met him?" someone asked.

"No. I am over that now."[269]

The room, including Hoch, laughed.

Hoch objected once. When Emilie said that Marie had asked her to do the washing because "he had been fooling around two or three days" with it, he leaned to Loftus and said, "That's a lie." He straightened up and curled his mustache to show he wasn't a man who let washing get away from him.

Later, he looked at Minnie Warnke, smiled, and told Loftus, "I loved her better than any of them."[270]

At noon, Hoch was annoyed when he learned he was to be taken to the Harrison Street station on the other side of the Loop to be photographed instead of being taken to lunch. His spirits were lifted on the way there when he saw a picture of Emilie outside of the Clark Street Dime Museum, where she had taken a job sitting onstage in "The Congress of Wives of Johann Hoch."

"That is a fine picture of Emilie, no?" he asked. "That will probably be more money for her. She is a great old girl, no?"[271]

At the station, he was photographed and measured. "Are you married?" asked the officer-in-charge.

"Yes, I am very much married," he said with a laugh.[272]

"You have quite large feet," said Captain Evans.

"They got that way going to and returning from New York," said Hoch. "I was doing the 'hot foot' you know."[273]

When all the measurements were taken, there was still plenty of time before the inquest was to resume. "Well," said Shippy, "I guess we can get a cup of coffee now and finish a small repast."

"I wish you'd make that coffee beer," said Hoch. "The coffee in Chicago is poor, but I can't kick on the beer!"[274]

Back in the inquest, Jacob Ness, a Cincinnati saloonkeeper, told of Hoch's two marriages there in 1896. He said he later heard Hoch had married another woman—probably Barbara Chuston—and then robbed and deserted her in Pennsylvania, but he had gotten away with it. Ness thought the property of a wife belonged to the husband.

"How do you know that?" asked the deputy coroner.

"I read a little once in a while," said (the misinformed) Ness.

"What is the law in Cincinnati?"

"That it closes at 12 o'clock."[275]

At one point, Hoch described Ness as "nothing but a hobo" and claimed never to have seen him. At other times, he said, "Mrs. Bartels Hoch died of kidney trouble. Of course the neighbors talked about the way the funeral was conducted. They didn't have anything else to do."[276]

This, of course, was an admission that he'd married Clara Bartels in the first place.

Mrs. Fischer was recalled to the stand to finish her story, telling how Marie had accused her of trying to steal her husband. "We quarreled, and she called me bad names. She said she did not care if I did marry her husband. I accused her of having left her former husband nineteen times and going to a dance while he was sick in a hospital."[277]

She repeated the story of Hoch, saying, "To the dead belong the dead, the living belong to the living," when Marie died.

"My, my, how nice," said Coroner Hoffman.

"Beautiful," said Hoch.[278]

The inquest was adjourned until the next Wednesday, which gave Hoch four full days of rest. He was taken to a restaurant, where he ordered a large meal and a black Havana cigar (it was reported that he paid for these luxuries himself, though what he was doing for money was never totally explained). Over dinner, he was told that letters had just brought stories of three more supposed wives. Hoch threw up his arms in frustration.

"How can I remember whether these women were my wives?" he asked. "I do not know them. If they had submitted a description of themselves I might have been able to tell whether I had ever seen them or married them, but with this letter business I am in the dark and will have to give up."[279]

One woman wrote that she had married "that devil" in June 1900. Hoch was in jail at the time.[280] Another letter said he had married a woman in

1887. Hoch denied that he'd been in the United States before 1895—one point on which he never wavered. Though Magerstadt occasionally claimed to have known him earlier, Hoch was probably telling the truth. On matters he was lying about, he usually slipped up eventually.

A correspondent for a Wisconsin paper asked Hoch about his Milwaukee wives.

"Nice beer there," he said. "I went there several times on the boat. No, I never married anybody in Milwaukee....The boat never stayed long enough." He told the reporter that he had nine wives and then immediately took it back. "Who told you there were nine?"[281]

Shippy told reporters, "[Hoch] is the most puzzling criminal the Chicago police have had to deal with in many years....Hoch will never confess he is a murderer. We will have to prove that—if we can—and he knows we'll have our hands full doing it."[282]

16

THE LADIES CAN'T RESIST YOU WHEN YOU LOOK LIKE JOHANN HOCH

Already convinced that Hoch wouldn't be tricked into confessing, Shippy tried a new tactic: coddling him.

Hoch slept in a comfortable bed in the police station. He was allowed to order his breakfast from a Clark Street restaurant—eggs, french fries, wheat cakes, and what the *American* called "odorous coffee."[283] Afterward, he let several reporters into Shippy's office to speak with him. When asked about the deaths of his wives, he said, "They might have died from a broken heart. But that does not make me culpable."[284]

Later, he asked to be taken to a barbershop. Shippy said he could recommend a first-class one nearby.

"Are they ladies?" Hoch asked.

"No," Shippy said. "I am afraid to trust you with a lady barber."[285]

He was escorted, unfettered by handcuffs, down the block to the barbershop in the majestic Bush Temple of Music building. "Now I think I want a massage," he said. "This jail life is ruining my complexion and there is a handsome little matron down there in the station that I want to marry."[286]

A rumor circulated that Hoch had already proposed to Alice Albrecht, the twenty-eight-year-old matron. He was said to have told her, "I will soon be out of this scrape. When I am I can make a barrel of money in a dime museum, and then we can be married and be happy I am sure."[287]

When asked about the proposal, Albrecht said, "Please do not joke with me. There is nothing to the story."[288]

A freshly-groomed Hoch with the men he said looked just like him. On the right is William Feller. Justice Mayer can be seen behind him. *Chicago Daily News. Chicago History Museum DN-0003590.*

Back in the station, freshly groomed, Hoch pointed out a couple of men around the jail who also had mustaches. "In order to prove to the public that other men look like me," he said, "I will consent to pose for a photograph, provided these two men will sit with me. If our pictures are printed in the newspaper I am satisfied that women will claim them as often as they claimed me."

He was duly posed, surrounded by Justice Theodore Mayer, Bailiff William Feller, and three other men.[289] The photo survives in the *Daily News* archives, though it wasn't printed in any surviving edition of a newspaper at the time. It wouldn't have proven Hoch's point very well, as none of the men looked much like him at all. A picture that had run in the *American* of Hoch with the mustached Shippy, Loftus, and Hoffman (page 109) would have been a more convincing argument. But Hoch was delighted by his models.

"You resemble in appearance a very handsome man," he told them with a laugh. "The ladies can't resist you when they know you look like Johann Hoch!"[290]

THE SUBJECT OF HYPNOTISM continued to come up, especially after Emilie Fischer came to the station, demanding that Hoch return her money. Hoch reportedly looked in her eyes and said, "Now here, my dear, don't get excited. I've got your money all right, and in good time you will get it all back and more, too."

"But John," she began.

Hoch placed a hand on her shoulder. "Now…you can't get anything by fighting me. If you make a row about it, it will all go to the lawyers before we get through. All these things they are saying about me are a pack of lies. I've got your money and I haven't stolen it. You go home and keep your mouth shut. I will discuss our affairs with you in private later on."

Fischer nodded and said, "All right, John," as Hoch was taken back into the "sweatbox." She waited by the door and finally a detective brought out a message: Hoch said, "I've said all I'm going to say today. Tell her to go home and shut up."

Fischer obediently left for home. The hypnotism angle may have been too much even for Shippy, but the change that came over Emilie Fischer certainly looked like hypnosis to reporters.[291]

ONE EVENING, HOCH WENT through his mail with detective Loftus. He had received a number of valentines and a great many proposals of marriage, some of which even seemed serious. Most were jokes. They both laughed at one signed "Carrie Nation," the name of a militant anti-liquor crusader, presumably sent by a pro-liquor joker who hoped Hoch would marry Carrie and murder her.

One was in original verse:

I'd rather be a widow, John, and free
From all the spells of Love, the young magician
Than marry you and know that I soon I'd be
A subject for the coroner's physician.

"Whoever wrote that would be a good enough wife for anyone," Hoch said. "I admire a woman who is clever. The trouble with all my wives was that they were stupid. I cared nothing for any of them. I marry them just the same as…What you call?…A business proposition? Yes. Certainly."[292]

While he read through the valentines, Hoch told Loftus some of his favorite epigrams that he hadn't had a chance to use on the train, such as, "A widow does not feel so sorry for the death of her first husband as her second husband does."[293]

Of his previous wives, he said, "All these women married me because they thought me wealthy, not because they loved me.…They gave me their money thinking to secure more. When they found themselves fooled, they turned on me like a pack of wolves."[294]

At one point in his confinement, Hoch told Detective Scribner that he made fifty dollars a week in the Pullman shops. "I gave Mrs. Goerk…$18 of this and led her to believe that was all my wages. It tickled her to think her devoted husband turned over all his earnings."[295]

Yet when the *Inter-Ocean* went to speak with Elizabeth Goerk, she was in a surprisingly forgiving mood. "I believe Hoch to be a perfect gentleman despite the charges against him," she said. "He was nice and an ideal husband. He was a man I was proud of and was not by any means a disgrace to me. I believe he is under the mysterious power of some woman."

Forgetting how many times she'd thwarted his schemes during their marriage, she went on to say, "He is not a mean criminal from his own motive. I tried often to study him and I failed to find anything bad in him.… [But] suddenly a change came over Johann. He became interested in some woman, I think. Maybe his former wife was following him and had located him in Chicago. Then he first mentioned a funny little passage which in German sounds much more sentimental: '*Zwei portemonaien—so was giebts bei urns nicht.*'"[296]

It translated to say, "Two wallets. We don't have anything like that."

17

TALES FROM THE MURDER CASTLE

People who'd been swindled kept coming to identify Hoch, but most left saying that he wasn't the man who'd robbed or deserted them, after all. Hoch was generally friendly with all of those who admitted their mistake, and he was also pleased to receive an old coworker from Pullman whom he did recognize. "Why, hello, Flycht," he said. "How are things down at the shops?"

"I just came to see, Schmitt, if you were really the man who worked beside me in the tin shops last year."

"Well, it's me all right....I recognize everyone I know who comes here. I am not trying to fool the police at all, but there are more people coming around here and identifying me whom I never saw before than you can shake a stick at."[297]

The witnesses who fascinated the press the most were those from the "H.H. Holmes Castle." "I know nothing about Holmes," Hoch told a reporter. "I have read about him in the papers, but that is all. I thought until Inspector Shippy told me Holmes was hanged in Philadelphia that he was hanged in Chicago."[298] But the rumors were loud enough that both the press and police investigated them fully—far more than they did many of the murders Hoch was accused of committing.

Evelyn Campbell was now picking up strands that she had left dangling when Hoch was captured, including her mystery "Castle" witness, whom she now revealed as one Anna Boyd. Boyd had lived around the corner and down the block from the Castle. Campbell brought her, heavily veiled, to

POLICE NOW SAY HOCK WAS A PUPIL OF BLUEBEARD HOLMES

Believe That Fugitive Was Guilty of Many of the Crimes Laid to the Englewood Man Ten Years Ago

Continued From First Page.

heard a word from them. I came to Chicago to look for my sister, but found no trace of her.

"My sister had with her $1,200 in money, a legacy from her first husband, and I suppose that it was this that made Hock anxious to marry her."

Gives New Evidence.

Benno Lechner, a saloonkeeper at 304 Larrabee street, put the police in possession of evidence that strengthens the case against Hock.

"In 1898," said Lechner, "I owned a saloon at 1320 Lincoln avenue, and Hoch (he called himself Heh then) had one at Milwaukee and Western avenues.

"In March of that year he married Mrs. Steinbrecher and the celebration was in my house.

"Two weeks afterward Hock came to me and told me that his wife was very sick and that he wanted $10 to buy medicine. I let him have it and went over to see Mrs. Heh. She was very sick and said:

"'That man is poisoning me.'

"I was just going to taste some of the medicine on the table when Heh came into the room and saw me.

"'Stop that!' he yelled, 'that is for the woman.'

"The next I heard was that Mrs. Heh was dead and that Heh had sold her property for nearly $4,000. He is the same man as in the photograph."

CITIZENS WAR TO-DAY ON EVIL OF DANCE HALL

Council Judiciary Committee to Hear Protests and Receive Draft of New Bill.

PROPRIETORS ARE COMBATIVE

The City Council Judiciary Committee this afternoon will be the center of an appeal by citizens representing half a dozen organizations who plan to check the dance hall evil.

The Law and Order League also will present a petition asking a repeal of the special permit to sell liquor after 1 a. m. and an amendment divorcing dancing from barrooms. It also will be suggested that the ordinance be further amended to provide for the exclusion of girls and women without escorts.

The dance hall proprietors, to counteract the petition, will be on hand with the draft of an ordinance much more stringent than any devised by the recognized reformers. A man who has a hall at Madison and Paulina streets submitted a copy of the proposed law to Inspector Wheeler and secured that official's approval of its provisions.

What the Proprietors Want.

The proprietors' measure reads as follows:

Dance Promoter—A person or persons who conduct one or more dances weekly for gain shall pay for privilege $500 a year. If liquors be sold at the dance a regular saloon license of $500 must be paid in addition to the former $500 dance license.

No liquor shall be sold in the dance hall proper; bar and serving room shall be a separate apartment. Minors shall not be admitted to dance halls where liquors are sold. The halls shall close, dance and bar, at 1 o'clock.

Special bar permits shall be issued only to chartered organizations on payment of $10 a day; privilege from 8 p. m. to 1 a. m., approved by Police Department.

Clubs and societies desiring to conduct a dance where admission is charged shall be required to pay $5 for a permit, application to be approved by license officer of Police Department.

The author of the measure told Inspector Wheeler that the proprietors of dance halls of the better sort were in favor of stringent regulations in order to save the reputations of their places.

[...]ENT OF RUSSIAN [...]KES FIRST STATEMENT

Copyright, 1905, by W. R. Hearst. [...]ondent of the Telegraph in St. [...] eighty prominent Russians, in[...]blicist Arsenieff, Messrs. Prugavin, [...]alled what they call a provisional [...]ing remarkable statement of their

[...] Russian traditions and pay inter[...]ofore negotiated, and leave noth[...] the curtailment of interest, or any [...]o the obligations undertaken by [...]

[...]racted after Sunday, January 22, [...], because no nation can now lend [...] faith or in ignorance of the fact [...]racy are struggling to determine [...]he nation.

[...] to support the autocracy, they [...] the Russian people will be equal[...]ons contracted by their enemies

Hoch shown alongside a portrait of J.C. Allen, a convict who had claimed he knew H.H. Holmes in 1895. Rumors were swirling that Hoch and Allen were one and the same. Also: a picture of the "Castle" as it looked in 1905 (with a pointed turret) and a mostly inaccurate diagram of its second floor. The bottom images show three Hoch wives (Mary Schultz turned out to be a false lead). *From the* Chicago American.

the station, where they found Shippy, Hoch, and Max Nootbaar, Shippy's secretary, in a large basement room.

Hoch greeted Evelyn warmly and then noticed her veiled companion and froze.

"There is the man," said Boyd. "That is Jake!"

And she dramatically threw back her veil.

Hoch held out his hands.

"I do not shake hands with such as you," she said.

"Here," said Hoch. "Let's have no more of this monkey business....Tell me at once; where did you see me?"

Boyd turned to Campbell. "Should I tell him?"

"Yes, tell him."

Anna Boyd trembled and then said, "I saw you in Holmes Castle!"

Hoch paused a moment before he gave a loud laugh. "That is all right," he said. "I have heard that yarn before. I am not afraid."

Boyd repeated her story and then said, "I don't know whether death will be my portion for all this, but at least I have done my duty."

Later that night, Evelyn brought in another witness, one William Brand, who had helped move stock around in the drugstore in the Castle building. He said he recognized Hoch from Englewood but admitted that he didn't recall seeing him in the castle.[299]

The next day, W.A. Slyter, who lived in the Castle building in 1892, was brought in and identified Hoch as "Jake Hect," a man who collected rents.[300] "I know you," he said to Hoch, "and you know me." Hoch called him a liar.[301]

Later, M.G. Chappel was brought in. Toward the end of the 1895 investigation of the Holmes Castle, police had introduced Chappel as the "articulator" who'd bought corpses from H.H. Holmes to turn them into skeletal models for medical schools. It became a part of Holmes's legend, but it had taken the newspapers only a day find that his story was nonsense. Chappel had been an articulator once, but long before Holmes was operating in Chicago. The police, coming under ridicule for an investigation that was going nowhere, had latched onto him, despite one paper dismissing his stories as "the vaporings of a weak mind." He hadn't been a reliable witness in 1895, and he kept up his streak a decade on.

"Yes, that's Jake," said Chappel, when he saw Hoch. "He was Holmes's financial agent. Handled all his property for him."[302] He said that Hoch was "the man" who had gone down to Fort Worth with Hoch and Pitezel in 1894 to build "The Minnie Williams Castle," another building on property that Holmes's girlfriend Minnie Williams had (according to the paperwork) sold to Holmes for one dollar around the time she disappeared.[303]

"What was Jake's last name?" asked Shippy. "Was it Hect?"

"No, his last name was Hoffman. Jake Hoffman."[304]

Chappel claimed to have pictures of Hoch inside of the building, and he brought in photos the next day. No one in the pictures resembled Hoch, and it's unlikely they were even from the Castle.[305]

Dr. E.H. Robinson, who'd run the drugstore in the castle building, spoke with Shippy for hours. "I never saw Hoch before," he said, "If he had been at the castle in any capacity from 1892 to 1894, I would have known him."

He also pointed out that the "missing man" who'd been part of the saga was named Hatch, not Hect. "I never heard of a Jake," he said, "Until Holmes [said] he had given the Pitzel children into the care of 'Jake Hatch,' and if they were murdered, 'Jake Hatch' killed them....He created 'Jake Hatch' out of whole cloth."[306]

There had, in fact, been stories in 1895 of a mysterious man who went to Texas with Holmes, and the *American* had even run drawing of him next to one of Hoch on January 24, suggesting that the two men might be one and the same, though even the drawings failed to look similar. That man, who had given a phony confession about his time with Holmes as part of a con, had been named John C. Allen and was known by several different aliases, but none of them was anything close to Jake Hoffman or Jake Hect, and he looked even less like Hoch than Mayer and Feller.

No one seemed to remember the details of the H.H. Holmes case very well at all in 1905, even the people who'd been connected to it. There'd been no major retelling of the story published to which people could have referred; all were just working from memory. And like the Hoch saga, the Holmes case had been such a tangle of shifting stories that anyone would have had a hard time figuring out what the real story was. Even Robinson, by far the most reliable witness among the Castle veterans, misremembered some details. The man Holmes had invented was named Edward Hatch, not Jake Hatch.

Shippy was fed up. "Here we have Mrs. Boyd declaring Hoch is Jake the Janitor," he said. "Now Slyter says that he is Jacob Hect, who he used to pay rent to, and Chappell says he is Jacob Hoffman." Shippy was now satisfied that Hoch really hadn't been in the country before 1895, far too late to have worked with H.H. Holmes.[307]

In Philadelphia, Franklin Geyer, the detective who'd discovered the bodies of three Holmes victims, said that the Hoch stories were "pure rot." "I suppose that echoes of the Holmes case will continue to bob up for the next twenty years," he groaned. "It makes me wish I had never heard of it."[308]

18

THE OLD JAIL

On Valentine's Day, Hoch was transferred from the East Chicago Avenue police station to the Cook County Jail, a droopy stone building that stood back to back with the courthouse.

The old jail was a curious place. Most of the prisoners were merely men awaiting trial; if convicted, they'd likely be sent to the state prison in Joliet. But those convicted of murder and sentenced to the gallows were also held there as they awaited execution, mingling freely with the other prisoners during exercise times. The jail would come to be known as a loose place; "trustees" were able to deliver all sorts of things to prisoners, and stories would eventually circulate of "love mills" and gambling rings. Jailer John Whitman, a quiet, sympathetic man, had asked the state to stop carrying out hangings in his jail altogether, but they would continue for more than twenty years.

"I suppose you have heard of our moral improvement association," Whitman told Hoch. "You had better become a member. It is a desirable organization here."

"It would give me a great deal of pleasure," Hoch said. "I will join at once unless there are formalities."

Whitman told him he should address the prison's society on some topic on which he was an expert. Hoch said he would and promised that it wouldn't be a predictable "Marriage Is a Failure" talk. "I will talk about something practical and interesting—perhaps my travels."[309]

A sketch of Hoch surrounded by his victims (plus Evelyn Campbell, who can be seen behind his chin). Though this is far more accurate than most similar montages, the man Ottumwa, Iowa madam Annie Pratt married was probably not Hoch. *From the* Chicago American.

Hoch was taken directly to cell 611 on the sixth floor, which was also Murderer's Row. He was not "coddled" there and was soon begging, in vain, to be taken back to the police station.

That afternoon, the *American*'s count of reported Hoch wives hit fifty.[310]

Hoch seemed to be in better shape for the next meeting of the inquest on February 15. After four days off, he was more alert, better groomed, and better dressed. "His stage presence is much improved," one official told a *Post* reporter.[311]

The most dramatic moment came when Hoch was shown a photograph of Marie Walcker's dead body. In the photo, she lay in a satin-lined casket, her hands crossed, her eyes closed, and her skin pale. The crowd in the room—mostly jurors, witnesses, and officials—watched closely, thinking that perhaps the photo would unnerve the prisoner. But Hoch, as he'd promised, was unmoved. "Yes," he said. "That was my wife."[312]

Mrs. Knipple, Marie's friend, spoke of attending the wedding of Johann and Marie.

"Did you kiss the groom?" asked the deputy coroner.

"No, I kissed the bride."[313]

Hoch laughed out loud at this.

Shippy said that Hoch had admitted to him that the fountain pen was his and that the substance inside was arsenic, though he said he'd planned to use it to die by suicide. He further stated that Hoch had confirmed a list of his activities over the past decade, which he read out as a "confession," listing several names of dead and deserted wives.[314] According to Shippy, Hoch had confessed to the following marriages:

Julia Steinbrecher, Chicago, August 1895
Minnie Warnke, Chicago, January 1896
Martha Hertzfeld, Chicago, January 1896
Caroline Hoch, Wheeling, September 1896
Clara Bartels, Cincinnati, March 1897
Maria Julia Doess, Cincinnati, Spring 1897
Elizabeth Goerke, Chicago, November 1901
Mary Becher, St. Louis, April 1902
Anna Hendricks, Chicago, January 1904
Marie Walcker, Chicago, September 1904
Emilie Fischer, Chicago, January 1905[315]

The dates he gave for them were off in many cases, and the list notably also didn't include Nannie Von Klenke, Caroline Streicher, the 1904 East Coast wives, or any of the wives from Hoch's spree in 1896–98.[316] But it also didn't contain any of the dozens of names that would turn out to be false positives.

Hoch would deny it all later that day. "I never told Inspector Shippy I had married eleven women," he said. "I signed a statement to the effect that I had not committed murder and that I was an innocent man. After that Mr. Shippy added six or seven pages of an alleged confession."[317] Such a trick would not have been out of character for Shippy, and the "confession" the inspector eventually read at the trial contained only cities and approximate dates—only Marie Walcker was mentioned by name.

The inquest could not yet be concluded, as the doctors had not yet given their full report on their investigations of Marie's body. Another meeting was scheduled for early the next week.

SHIPPY NOW TOLD REPORTERS that Emilie Fischer was a suspect herself.

"I have believed all along that Mrs. Fischer had guilty knowledge that her sister did not die a natural death," he told the *Journal*. "This was but the climax of a long enmity between the sisters. Mrs. Bertha Sohn, a third sister, testified at the inquest that Mrs. Fischer had won Mr. [Emil] Walcker, Mrs. Walcker's first husband, and had lived with him two months openly after he had left his wife. If I were a member of the coroner's jury I should vote…to bind Mrs. Fischer over to the grand jury as an accessory to her sister's murder."[318]

If Bertha told that story, it made shockingly little news and was never expanded on, which makes it seem like typical hot air from Shippy. But lawyer Plotke alluded to it as well—and as Marie's divorce lawyer, he would have been in a position to know. Plotke now suggested to reporters that he agreed with Shippy: Emilie had poisoned Marie herself in order to steal her second husband, too. "A bowl of soup will figure in the evidence," he said. "And the question of who cooked and served the soup will prove interesting."[319]

Shippy also noted that Mrs. Fischer had given up on trying to get money back from Hoch and had even been to his office to get a good picture of him.[320] It was briefly mentioned in the press that Emilie had hired a lawyer named Michael Hunt. No such lawyer is listed in the city directory for that year, so it may be a case of a *Journal* reporter falling for a dirty joke. Perhaps Hoch had told him that Emilie had hired "Mike Hunt."[321]

For his part, Hoch wished he could go back to staying at the police station and continued his crusade against the coffee in Chicago.

"The meals here [in jail] are fierce," he said. "And they will not allow me to sleep in the morning. I was told this morning that if I did not get up at 7 o'clock I would get no breakfast and would be allowed no exercise. I got up and, what a breakfast! Coffee and rolls. The coffee was bad, the rolls were worse."[322]

Hoch refused to speak to Evelyn Campbell further after her "Castle" accusation, which had been a misstep on her part. She closed out her coverage of the case by visiting the museum where Emilie Fischer was appearing onstage. The "act" consisted of her sitting in a rocking chair.

"[She] carries the weight and age which make a rocking chair appear her most fitting environment," Campbell wrote of the fifty-two-year-old Emilie. "She has for general counsellor, guide, and interpreter Lulu, the tattooed lady, who sits with her, and she is flanked on either side by Little Bear, Cherokee Chief, and a bevy of young women who are singing songs and things in a popularity contest."[323]

"Ach!" Fischer told her. "I'd rather scrub."

Campbell eyeballed a man in the crowd who looked like a farmer, slack-jawed and staring. "I began to see his gray matter convulate," she wrote. The man thought with all his might and finally came up with what he considered a witty remark: "Say, if you're a sample, I'm going up to bail Hoch out."

He was led away by a stage manager but was replaced in the crowd by what Campbell called "two girls whom I'll match as the champion gigglers against any pair in existence."

"He he he, isn't she too cunning?" laughed one.

"I'll bet Hoch's just awful lonesome without her," said the other.

Fischer spoke to Campbell through the tattooed lady.

"It's like this all day," Fischer said. "All the foolish men and women in Chicago come here and talk like that. Do you wonder I'd rather scrub?"

"I've never been a dime museum attraction at $250 a week," Campbell wrote. "But I have scrubbed, and, well—I had my doubts."

Reports of Hoch's past crimes kept surfacing, but more and more often, they turned out to be mistakes. About a week after Hoch was brought back to Chicago, the police arrested a man named Frank Busch, another mustached German man who'd been running matrimonial scams. Immediately, it became clear that some of the people who'd identified Hoch as the man who'd swindled them had really been swindled by Frank Busch. Hoch was elated, and Busch himself was reportedly pleased to hear he resembled Hoch.

But clearing up this handful of false accusations didn't matter much, as they weren't at issue in the current case. On February 23, two weeks after Hoch arrived in Chicago, the coroner's inquest held its final meeting.

Dr. Walter Haines issued his final report: arsenic had been found in Marie Walcker's liver, stomach, and kidneys, including 7.6 grains in her stomach—far more than enough to kill a person. They also noted that no arsenic had been used in the embalming fluid.[324]

Hoch, on the advice of Plotke, did not take the stand in his own defense.

The coroner's jury indicted him for murder, and a grand jury would follow days later.

Hoch said he agreed with the analysis but was counting on a test to show the coroner was mistaken when he said there was no arsenic in the embalming fluid. "Does anyone think," he said, "if I am the cunning poisoner they try to make me out, that I would give my wife enough poison to kill a horse?...I do not think any jury will believe that I ever committed so bungling a crime as that."[325]

19

ON TRIAL

In 1889, a white drifter named Nat Oliphant was lynched in Topeka by a mixed-race mob estimated to number ten thousand—about one-third of the town's population. Among the witnesses was a young law student, Harry Olson, the future Illinois state's attorney who would prosecute Johann Hoch in court.[326]

Olson's views on what transpired that night are not recorded, though one can imagine that he disapproved based on the fact that he later hired Ida B. Wells, the noted anti-lynching advocate, as a probation officer. Like many in his profession, he viewed judicial capital punishment as an important measure to keep citizens from resorting to mob justice.

He believed that Hoch—and nearly every other criminal he fought to have executed—suffered "dementia praecox," a disorder that would now be diagnosed as schizophrenia. Though he admitted that the public appetite did now allow for forced sterilization of such people, he believed that at the very least, these individuals should be sent to farm colonies.[327] Olson was later president of the Eugenics Research Association, which advocated improving society by regulating, or at least influencing, who could and couldn't reproduce. He rejected the racism pervasive to the field (indeed, Chicago's Black newspapers were known to call him him a champion of racial justice),[328] and many of his writings on the subject wouldn't even be considered "eugenics" today—support for contraception and social and economic reforms that could de-emphasize the need to marry and have a family (the sort of conditions that led so many women to marry Johann

THESE ACCUSING HANDS POINT TO HOCH!

"BIGAMIST" IS THEIR CRY

WIVES TO CONFRONT SLAYER

MRS. RANKIN-HOCH. MRS. HENDRICKSEN-HOCH. MRS. FISHER-HOCH.

These three women claim to be wives of Johann Hoch, whose trial for wife-murder began to-day. They will be important witnesses for the state.

State's Attorney's Office Acts Promptly to Prevent Flaw in the Original Presentment.

Johann Hoch, arch-bigamist and accused slayer of many wives, was placed on trial to-day before Judge Kersten, after the state, by a sensational move in the eleventh hour, frustrated a clever plot to free the defendant on a technicality.

On April 18, the *American* ran what it called a photo from the trial. It had pasted a photo of Minnie Warnke, likely taken on February 10, onto a shot taken of Hendricks and Fischer at the February 1 inquest. That newspaper photos were often mock-ups, or retouched for publication, was by no means a secret, though how well the general public understood it is debatable. *From the* Chicago American.

Hoch) were all lumped in with eugenics at the time.[329] But Olson seemed irresponsibly, even willfully, ignorant to how race would likely be used in determining who was and wasn't "defective" if some of the measures he advocated for were adopted.

By every account, Olson was a sharp prosecutor. One lawyer said that while battling him in court, "You will be congratulating yourself on the way your case is going, until you chance to see a pool of blood on the floor, when you will realize suddenly, 'That's my blood!'"[330]

It was announced in the press that Edmund Furthmann would represent Hoch at the trial. A veteran lawyer who'd been an assistant prosecutor against the Haymarket anarchists, Furthmann had some experience in chemistry and had recently been working as successful defense lawyer. He'd taken on accused murderers whose fondest hope was a mere life sentence, not the gallows, and helped them walk out free.[331] He could have been a worthy match for Olson. However, when the trial came, Hoch was still represented by the hapless Isadore Plotke. Again, the fact that Plotke had been Marie Walcker's divorce lawyer was not mentioned.

Olson and Plotke had gone against each other in front of Judge Kersten a year earlier, when Plotke defended Emil Roeski, who was on trial for the murder of one Otto Bauder as part of a gang of criminals known as the Car Barn Bandits. Plotke had claimed his client had been "hypnotized" into joining the gang and killing Bauder, and he requested permission to do hypnotic experiments on him in his cell to show he was an easy subject. Whitman turned him down.

The hypnosis angle hardly seemed necessary in that case, given that another of the bandits had already confessed to killing Bauder. But Plotke lost anyway. He did save him from execution, though, and the conviction was hardly his fault; the case had been so highly publicized that it was unlikely that *any* evidence in Roeski's favor would have been enough for an acquittal. The Hoch case was just as famous, and now Plotke had less evidence in his favor to work with. The odds were against him in every way.

After days of jury selection, Olson opened his case with a small revelation: Marie's body had been disinterred again the previous week, and tests had shown (again) that the embalming fluid used on her remains contained no arsenic.

Hoch jumped up and blurted out something that sounded like "What is that?"[332]

It would prove to be the most dramatic moment of a three-week trial that seemed most shocking for its blandness. It received relatively little coverage in the papers, given what a sensation Hoch had been three months before. The proceedings were mostly a recitation of the same stories that had been told at the inquests, with the addition of New York police and a few other local witnesses telling their stories. Hoch was photographed falling asleep during the testimonies.

Evelyn Campbell took the stand to summarize a little of what Hoch had told her on the train.

Of the many wives, only Emilie Fischer would be called as a witness; the courts cited Caroline Streicher of Philadelphia as Hoch's most recent wife, which rendered the other Chicago wives irrelevant. Stories of past wives, including the convincing stories that he'd murdered four others, could not be used at the trial.

But other local wives continued to show up at the court, sometimes "in gay Easter attire."[333] On the second day of jury selection, four of the wives—Minnie Warnke, Elizabeth Goerk, Anna Hendricks, and Emilie Fischer—were all said to be in attendance, chatting pleasantly with one another. Warnke carried an American beauty rose and was seen to give Hoch knowing smiles. Hoch smiled back at her at one point, thinking that she was giving him the flower, but she held it, using it as a symbol only she understood.[334]

One day early in the trial, Fischer lost her umbrella. "First that man takes all my money," she said, "and now, when I come to see him punished, I lose my umbrella. He is bad luck to me."[335]

BEHIND THE SCENES, THERE was a battle taking place for Emilie Fischer's loyalty.

Early in his confinement, Fischer met with Hoch on multiple occasions. He assured her that the state had no real evidence against him and that after he was released, they could work in museums together. In a year or two, they'd have enough money to be set for life. She told him she stood the risk of being called an accomplice if she changed what she'd said at the inquest, but Hoch assured her that everything would be all right. She asked him to swear and promise by all that was holy that he hadn't killed her sister, and he did.

When she lost her apartment on Wells Street early that spring, Fischer was sent to live with Officer Fisher, a policeman who spoke German. With the officer's help, Shippy and Olson worked to convince her that Hoch was a murderer who was now lying to her. They likely told her that if she didn't testify against him, they could make it look as though *she* was the killer. They kept her from seeing Hoch again and likely kept her from Plotke as well. After all, Plotke's plan to do "hypnotic experiments" on his previous client suggested that he knew how to hypnotize people.

Shippy and Olson's work paid off. On the stand in the trial, Fischer said that she didn't believe all the stories that had been told of Hoch but repeated her now-familiar stories of her fight with Marie, Marie's death, and Hoch's morbid courtship: "To the dead belong the dead, to the living belong to the living."

Neither the state nor Plotke pursued their early plan to hold her as an accomplice. When she was asked, briefly, if she'd given her sister arsenic, Emilie said, "Kindly do not ask such foolish questions."

Plotke's own star witness, Dr. Gustav Kolischer, stated that if there were 7.6 grams of arsenic placed in a stomach during life, that stomach would be in far worse shape than Marie Walcker's had been. In his opinion, the arsenic must have been placed there after her death.

This could have been a damaging opinion, but Plotke gave a terribly ham-fisted response. He began asking Kolischer if it was true that cemetery dirt could be contaminated with arsenic, and when Kolischer confirmed that it could, Plotke suggested that the arsenic had seeped into the coffin in the few days before Marie was exhumed. Kolischer hadn't meant to suggest this and was deeply embarrassed to have his testimony used to suggest something so ludicrous.[336]

Plotke also suggested that the arsenic came from the wallpaper in the cottage. Many defense lawyers had tried that in the years since the dangers of wallpaper that used arsenic for color became known, but it never worked—and didn't work this time.

He then suggested that perhaps the arsenic had been planted by the police or coroner. This wasn't impossible, but he failed to push the issue effectively.

Even if the arsenic in the stomach *had* been added after death, it came out at the trial that the fatal dose may not have been mixed into anything Marie drank; instead, it may have been mixed into her enemas and administered rectally. When the nurse had given her enemas of solutions she had prepared herself, Marie seemed to get better. When the nurse was dismissed, and Emilie and Bertha had had administered solutions Hoch prepared, she got worse. This wasn't widely reported in public but may have been persuasive to the jury.

Nurse Holzapfel testified that Dr. Reese had told her to administer enemas as needed, but Reese said he had not told Hoch to give Marie any enemas at all.

Through it all, Hoch sat mostly motionless. He never took the stand.

WHEN THE CASE CONCLUDED, every reporter heard Hoch turn to one of Plotke's assistants. "I will bet you that I will be acquitted," he said.

"I would not bet on a man's life," came the reply.[337]

The *Tribune* wrote that "the evidence…did not seem altogether conclusive."[338] The state's whole premise seemed overly complicated. Marie didn't have much money—why murder her when he could have simply deserted her, as he had done so many times before? The state believed he had killed Marie to get the slightly wealthier Emilie to marry him, but that would have been a risky move, given how frequently his proposals were turned down—unless Emilie had, in fact, made an arrangement with him ahead of time.

But the jury was back in just two hours with its verdict: guilty, with the penalty fixed at death.

As he was led away, Hoch looked at the jury and said, "Well, I guess it's all up with John."[339]

The only Hoch wife present that day was Emilie Fischer, who "spoke in a whirlwind of German, shaking her fist at the doorway where Hoch disappeared." "He has told me often that he could beat anyone, the very best of them," she said. "Now I guess he finds out there are better ones than he is. He could fool foolish women, maybe, but not so many men. He killed my sister, now they kill him. That is good and it is right."[340]

The sentiment was echoed elsewhere. Back around Mohawk Bridge in Cincinnati, people celebrated at Ness's saloon and said it was "the most eminently respectable thing" they'd ever heard about "Old Schmitt Hoch."[341]

Back in his cell, Hoch smiled for reporters. "It is so beautiful to go to one's death with an innocent conscience," he said. "I am innocent of killing my dear, dear wife. She died a natural death, but Olson has got his verdict, and so it's all right. He has hung Johann, and I wish the verdict would be carried out at once—in half an hour!"

A moment later, he dropped a bombshell: "[Marie] committed suicide," he said. "She bought rat poison, and gave it to herself."[342]

This was a more reasonable explanation than much of what Plotke had come up with.

Plotke, for his part, announced that he would ask for a new trial but admitted that he couldn't explain the fountain pen full of arsenic. "That was hard evidence to get around," he told a reporter. "I cannot say I am surprised at the verdict in view of the evidence the state introduced, but I expected a penitentiary sentence."[343]

The next morning, Hoch arose in his cell after what appeared to be a peaceful sleep. He had breakfast and exercised in the jail corridor.[344]

"Say," he said, "where there's life there's hope, and Johann Hoch is still alive, ain't he? Yes, you bet."[345]

20

A NEW REPORTER ENTERS THE SAGA

In 1888, a London paper ran a series of articles titled "Is Marriage a Failure?" The question became a catchphrase—Hoch referred to it regularly—and inspired a title for a popular play. One couple who performed the play on stage in the United States was a pair of actual newlyweds, Frederick Renolds and Jean Cowgill.

Cowgill was born in Kankakee, Illinois, two days before the Great Chicago Fire broke out sixty miles north. She was raised mainly in the Black Hills of South Dakota, where, according to an early profile, "her nursemaids were cowboys." She spent two years as a schoolmarm on a reservation before marrying young and embarking on a stage career.

In 1893, the year she and Renolds were performing *Is Marriage a Failure?* (which, in their case, it turned out to be), Cowgill took a side job as a correspondent for the *Chicago Times.*[346] Journalism, she later wrote, was "about the only profession where women get their deserts without any argument or lowering of either prices or self-respect."[347]

By 1902, now a newly divorced single mother, Cowgill writing for a number of papers. She would always recall a particularly eventful couple of months that year when she interviewed Thomas Edison, Lord Kelvin, and Guglielmo Marconi, the inventor of the wireless telegraph. Marconi told her that one day there would be "pocket editions" of telephones that people would carry around with them and use to call anyone in the world without wires.[348] At the end of 1903, she was commended for her firsthand reporting on the Iroquois Theatre fire.

By 1905, she had moved away from regular reporting to magazine features on every subject from labor relations to clairvoyance (she was a great supporter of "new thought" ideas about psychic powers, telepathy, and hypnosis). Her biggest ongoing project was a weekly series for the *Chicago Chronicle*'s Sunday pullout magazine titled "Perils of a Great City," in which she exposed the threat to public morals held by dance halls, chop suey joints, and even ice cream parlors (in all cases, they were places where impressionable young women might gather without chaperones). The articles were, by turns, both progressive and stuffy, but they were always engaging and usually accompanied by stylish illustrations by Dan Sayre Groesbeck, who would go on to create concept art for Cecil B. DeMille.

In many articles, she renounced the wilder days of her youth, saying they'd brought her nothing but pain. But in early 1905, rumor had it that Cowgill had been caught in a closet making out with a young *Chronicle* reporter,[349] and she was definitely dating a lawyer several years her junior at the time.

In June that year, she interviewed Johann Hoch in his cell for a *Chronicle* feature.

Hoch had been scheduled to hang at the end of the month, but Cowgill found him laughing, at least at first. She noted that Hoch's high voice had a musical quality to it. As he sat, he "clasped and unclasped his spatulate-ended fingers."

"Why should I be hanged?" he asked her. "The man who did it should be. I would be wicked to say that I think any one did it. That is what the state has done with me. What do you think that state pays for? Do you think it is to find men innocent or guilty or only to convict?"

Cowgill had to admit that she'd often asked herself the same question.

"Mr. Olson wrote a nice little dime novel with the evidence that he found," Hoch went on. "No poor man can have a fair trial."

"Why did you marry the next wife so soon?" Cowgill asked him.

"It looks bad, doesn't it?" asked Hoch. "It was my wife who was sick who made me promise to marry [Emilie]....[Marie] spoke that way for two days before she died."

"Did you love her?"

"Of course I loved her. I have traveled a great deal. I wanted a home."

And then he went into yet another version of his early history, now claiming to be French, not German. "My great-grandfather fought with the great Napoleon," he said. "He was General Louis Hoch. When Napoleon was exiled to St. Helena my grandfather went along. He was with him when he died."

Bluebeard Hoch Under Death Sentence

(BY JEAN COWGILL.)

A NOVEL, that is what it is!" Johann Hoch laughed sarcastically. He was in ler Whitman's office in the county l.

t was his trial that he was talking ut. "It was a novel. Think of it this: Take a cook stove that you e in one corner. In another corner is radle. Give those to some rascally iter and say: 'Write me a novel.' u know what I think of my trial. I e no one to blame—not one. Only I that it is not fair to convict a man something that never happened."

he pictures of Hoch do not do him tice. He is a very good example of intelligent foreigner.

loch's head is wide and massive. ybe it is inclined to be a little bul-shaped. His eyes are gray and n-expressioned. When he came wn to talk to me he wore a good t of black clothes and immaculate en. He looks like a man who has ways been accustomed to the good ngs of life.

Tell me the story," I said. He did it idily.

Hoch Tells His Story

I was in New York," he said. "I d in the papers that a man was nted for bigamy. I made up my nd that I would not face that charge. I went out to a drug store and ught 10 cents' worth of arsenic. I s going to kill myself. Then I saw next day that the man they wanted s Johann Hoch and that I was rged with the murder of my wife. st settled me. I went straight to the rty-seventh street police station and ked to the officer there. I had the per with me. 'See this picture?' I id. 'It does not look like me, but I the man. I am Johann Hoch. I nt to start to Chicago tonight.'"

Hoch leaned toward me a little. His eech was impassioned. So that those the outside of the office might not ar Jailer Whitman closed the door. och clasped and unclasped his atulate-ended fingers. They are y well cared for too. Hoch has a ft voice; even when it is loudest ere are strains that are musical in it. ere are few lines on his face and tle that seems low. The more one ks with him the more of a paradox becomes.

He almost shouted the next words, t there was still that strain of softss and sweetness in his voice.

"You now know what they did. They ade it as hard as they could for me have a new trial. Before I was tried said like this," Hoch held up his two oad hands and counted the fingers as spoke. "There is my wife. She says at I did not kill her sister, so she nothing. The nurse knows that I did t give my other wife anything all e time that she was there. She can t say that I killed her. Dr. Reese ys that my wife died of Bright's disse, so he cannot say that I killed her. w, who can?"

He paused dramatically. "Who did?" asked triumphantly. "Who did? hy, the undertaker that embalmed

Groesbach's illustration accompanying Jean Cowgill's article on Hoch (shown here from an Indiana paper's abridged version of the article, published long after the original). The original ran in the *Chicago Chronicle. From the* Chicago Chronicle.

To other reporters that week, Hoch had claimed he was the grandson of Michel Ney, another of Napoleon's aides, which several newspapers noted couldn't possibly have been true. Papers in Germany thought it was hilarious; the Schmidts had been in Horrweiler for generations.

But something in Hoch struck a chord in Cowgill.

Left in a thoughtful state by her interview, she went to speak with a couple of lawyers. The first asked her if she minded if he smoked a cigar. She didn't mind a bit, though she noted for her readers that smoking was fine for men, but an awful habit for women.

"Let me tell you," said the lawyer as he puffed on the big, black cigar, "that if Hoch had taken the stand in his own behalf he would never have been convicted. Let them do what Hoch says: prove who did it."

She also interviewed a judge who seemed to agree with her that hanging was a worse murder than any other. "When a man is hanged," he said, "it is the result of a deliberate conspiracy on the part of the state."

Another lawyer—quite possibly the one Cowgill was dating—told her, "I don't think that a man should be hanged just because he married a lot of silly women. That is bigamy and not murder. I followed the evidence pretty closely and I don't think he killed that woman....I want to see that sentence stayed and that man given a new trial."

"Hoch says he is not a bigamist," Cowgill noted.

The lawyer only laughed. "That is where he is mistaken," he said. "He is undoubtedly a bigamist. That crime he should confess to and be cleared of the other."

"Do you believe in hanging?" she asked.

"Who that is civilized does? If I had my way I wouldn't destroy the life of a fly."

Cowgill already didn't believe in hanging, and now, she decided that she didn't believe Johann Hoch was guilty. She wouldn't write about him as much as Evelyn Campbell had, but she would stay with the case until the end.

21

TO BEAT THE GALLOWS

Cowgill buried an important bit of news at the end of her feature: Emilie Fischer had forgiven Hoch and now insisted that he was innocent.

"Tremblingly, the woman creeps to the jail to see him," Cowgill wrote. "She cries and justifies him when she comes. 'He married me to take care of me,' she says. 'He did not kill my sister.'"

Days later, the *Daily News* picked up on this turn of events as well. Mrs. Fischer had started working to save Hoch and was traveling around trying to raise money for his cause.[350]

At the trial, Fischer had been unconvincing in her claims that Hoch hadn't begun courting her before Marie died. She'd admitted to destroying all of the letters Hoch had sent her, and when asked what they'd spoken about in the Union Avenue cottage, besides his late former wife, she tried to dodge the question, eventually saying, "We talked about one thing and another." She did admit that one night, when Hoch walked her to the train car, he'd said, "Sister-in-law, if I had met your four weeks sooner, I would have married you."

On June 21, with two days to go until the scheduled hanging, Hoch told reporters that everything would be fine, that he was the "happiest man in jail," though reporters said that he was starting to seem nervous, and Plotke was telling him there was no hope.[351]

Plotke was impressing nobody. When R. Keene Ryan of the *American* and a photographer went to see Hoch in his cell, Plotke came up to Ryan and whispered, "Get me in that picture. It's about all that I will ever get out of this affair."[352]

Ryan, certain that Plotke meant that he was only in it for the advertising, was disgusted.

A neighbor on murderer's row, Joseph "Jocko" Briggs, was scheduled to be hanged the same day as Hoch. Briggs, too, had people working to get him a new trial, but he had one ally Hoch didn't: Evelyn Campbell. Campbell had been off the Hoch case since her article on Emilie's museum act; during the spring, she'd written about a man who claimed his wife's Ouija board had turned her against him, about efforts to stop parents from making children say prayers that said "if I die before I wake" before bed, and about psychic sisters who were making a fortune in "spirit paintings" before starting work on the Jocko Briggs case. She believed that Briggs was innocent. In late June, as the execution date approached, she told another reporter, "Three nights in succession, I slept in the office in a chair. I have worked day and night for [Briggs], in whom I had no interest whatever until I became convinced he had been jobbed by the police."[353]

The night before the scheduled execution, both men got a reprieve. Briggs was granted a new trial, and Hoch was given a reprieve until July 28 to give him more time to find a way to get his case in front of the state supreme court. At noon the next day, the time that they were supposed to be hanged, Hoch and Briggs met in the prison barbershop.

"Hello, Jocko!" said Hoch. "How are you feeling?"

"Fine as a fiddle and confident as a lion. How about you, John?"

"I never felt better in my life. But say, Briggs, it was a pretty good nerve trainer, wasn't it?"

"The worst ever," said Briggs.

"But you didn't get the fright I did," Hoch went on. "Say, I thought [Governor] Deneen was cold-blooded, but he seems to be just the opposite. He certainly gave Johann Hoch a chance for life!"[354]

A letter to the *Chicago Daily News* railed against the sympathy for both men, which the writer said was due to "hysterical female reporters" like Evelyn Campbell.[355]

Jocko Briggs would go on to be acquitted, and Campbell would often be credited with saving him from the gallows.

But she had no intention of helping Johann Hoch.

On July 23, the *American* ran an article in its Sunday magazine titled "How I Married 50 Women and What Became of Them," credited to Hoch himself, as dictated to a reporter.

"The night I was born," it quoted Hoch as saying, "my mother dreamed that the devil appeared in the room and, pointing at me, laughed and said, 'This child is cursed.'"

The article was full of thrilling tales. At one point, Hoch claimed to have bought a Cripple Creek mine for $45,000. When the mine turned out to be useless, he melted the nuggets of fools' gold down into bullets and used them to shoot one of the men who'd tricked him. "They tell me he is carrying one of them now in his hip joint."

But most of the long piece told of Hoch's "matrimonial investments," beginning in his youth in Bingen, where he eavesdropped on hundreds of men proposing at a popular romantic spot and learned that "love is a game of war." He gave tips on wooing women—including things like claiming to be an anarchist assassin, or the reincarnation of Goethe or Jack the Ripper.

Perhaps the stories came from the manuscript Hoch said he was writing (which was to be called *Hoch, the Life and Adventures of Johann Hoch, a Traveler in Many Lands, With Many Interesting Experiences*), but it's more likely that the entire

How I Married 50 Wives and what Became of them

—As told by Johann Hoch, the Professional Bridegroom and Wholesale Murderer in an Amazing History of His Life while Awaiting His Execution in Chicago

My Matrimonial Investments.

Chapter I.

Chapter II.

Chapter III.

Chapter IV.

List of Hoch's 50 Wives.

"I watched at the bedside of each of my unfortunate wives with tenderest devotion."

The Hoch "confession" that ran in the *American*'s Sunday pullout magazine. Hoch denied having anything to do with it, and he was likely telling the truth. *From the* Chicago American.

article was completely phony. At no point in the long narrative does it sound like Johann Hoch talking, and it's not something *anyone* would have written while trying stave off an execution scheduled for the next week. Around the article were portraits of several wives, but the captions weren't accurate. The same Mary Becher photo was used for both "May Gardner" and "Lulu Dotz." Anna Hendricks appeared as both herself and "Mary Becke."

Few likely took the article seriously. It was, after all, a part of the *American*'s Sunday pullout magazine. Even in the less dramatic papers, Sunday pullouts tended to resemble the tabloids that would line supermarket checkout lanes later in the century. Hoch, for his part, disavowed the article completely. In a letter to the *Chicago Journal*, he stated, "I never wrote, dictated, nor inspired a sentence to the story." For once, he might have been telling the truth.

In a parting shot, he added, "If the *Chicago American* would like something really 'shocking,' why not let it print the story of how it gave Evelyn Campbell a pocket full of gold pieces, which she offered me in the Chicago Avenue police station after exhausting other wiles for a confession….I place all the blame for my fate upon the *Chicago American*."

The *Journal* printed Hoch's letter in full. It had certainly never said anything to suggest Hoch was innocent, but it never missed a chance to let somebody criticize the *American*.[356]

22

JUSTICE FOR THE POOR

In July, the *Journal* ran headline after headline attacking Chief O'Neill, blaming him for all the crime in the city. O'Neill would resign by the end of the month, replaced by John Collins, who would last only a couple of years before he was put on trial for corruption.

As August approached, word got around that Hoch hadn't been able to raise enough money for an appeal. It wasn't for lack of trying; he'd even organized a prize fight between two jail guards who had formerly been boxers as a fundraiser.[357] But the *American* reported that Hoch was still $372 short of the funds needed to take his case to the state supreme court. Beginning to grow desperate, he threatened to destroy the manuscript he was working on.

"If I am hanged," he said, "the world will be cheated. I will tear every page to bits, to confetti, you understand? The public will have to suffer by the loss of the greatest literary achievement since the Bible."[358]

Twenty-four hours before the rescheduled execution, the "death watch" officially began. Hoch was brought to the "death chamber," the relatively comfortable room where condemned men slept the night before they were to be hanged. Comfortable though it was, prisoners could hear the hammer as the gallows were constructed in the jail's north corridor (they were taken apart and rebuilt for each hanging). Hoch paced the cell to the rhythm of the hammers all afternoon.[359]

"You people scorn Russia," he said. "They never hang men there for lack of money. They exile them for crimes proven. Here in the state of Illinois your courts are crazy for convictions."[360]

Just before dinner time, Plotke returned to tell Hoch he'd again failed to find the money to get the case before the state supreme court. "It is useless to fight any longer," he said. "You must be hanged."

"It is not useless," Hoch told him. "I will not be hanged until tomorrow. You get out of here and get that money before that time, and I'll not die."

"Where shall I get it?" Plotke asked.

"I don't know!" Hoch roared. "Rob someone. Kill a millionaire. Get it somehow."

"Hoch," Plotke said, "You should now think of the life to come.…Make ready to meet your creator."

"Coward," said Hoch.[361]

But while Plotke had given up, other people hadn't. Nearly everyone agreed with Hoch that it is was an outrage that he would be executed because he was a few hundred dollars short.

The next morning, Francis McNamara, the county physician, told the *American*, "If that man hangs today it will be a disgrace to the city of Chicago, the laws, and the people of the state of Illinois. Eliminating all question of Hoch's guilt or innocence.…Money ought not to stand in the way of a man securing his full legal rights."[362]

Even state's attorney Olson said he would like to see a reprieve. "I think there should be a law," he said, "which would enable a condemned man to appeal his case to the supreme court if he so desired, and the state should pay the expense in case the person is without funds."[363] Bills to that effect had been proposed, but stalled in state government.

It was raining hard by dawn on the morning of his scheduled execution, and as Hoch dressed for what was to be his final morning, he looked out the window.

"Did you ever see such weather? Look at the sky. It is black! Nature is weeping for me."[364]

Meanwhile, there was a man named Dr. Liston Montgomery who had examined the case, interviewed Hoch, and determined that Marie Walcker had died of Bright's disease. He read of Hoch's lack of funds that morning during his ride to work. "By the time I reached my office," he later said, "my mind was made up and I immediately called Plotke on the telephone."[365]

He also called Cora Wilson, a Wabash Avenue fur dealer who'd helped prisoners before. By 9:30 a.m., she and Dr. Montgomery were in a phone conference with Governor Deneen, who asked the sheriff to delay the execution from noon to 1:00 p.m. Since the sentence specified that he should be hanged "between 10 and 2," this could be done without any paperwork.

In his cell, Hoch seemed calm. When noon came and went, he looked to the guards and said, "What did I tell you?" Whitman then came to inform him he had an extra hour. Hoch lit a cigar and put his feet on the table. "This just bears out my contention that I'll never hang," he said.

But he fidgeted nervously with the flowers he'd been given that morning.

Meanwhile, attorney Albert Thompson phoned Plotke with a promise of $500.

"If that offer is made in good faith, Thompson, I can get a reprieve," he said.

"I'll be right over in a cab," Thompson said.[366]

What followed was a farce of opening and closing doors and of cabs driving back and forth to offices, banks, and the Sherman Hotel, where a teleconference with the governor was set up. With no time to spare, various forces were conspiring to get the money and inform the governor.

Albert Thompson arrived at the jail, check in hand, but the state's attorney said he couldn't take a personal check that large. So, Thompson, now with Plotke in tow, hopped into a cab and rushed to the Hibernian Bank in the Loop at Clark and Monroe. Inside, they found a long line at the teller's window.

Thompson pushed right through the line, shouting, "I am after $500 to save Johann Hoch's life! I can't wait, I must have the money now!"[367]

The *American* would put out at least eleven editions about Hoch that day as the dramatic scene unfolded. Noon and early afternoon editions screamed out, "Hoch's Nerve Breaking" and "They Murder Me, Cries Hoch." An extra edition shouted, "Hoch Gets Hour More," and a further extra said, "Pledge Hoch Life Money."

At 12:40 p.m., twenty minutes before Hoch was to have been taken from the cell to be hanged, word came that the governor was assured that the various parties had come up with the funds, and he was sending a telegram to the sheriff granting another four-week reprieve.

Frank Comerford, a young lawyer and politician, had been running around the courthouse building frantically, starting up a subscription to raise the necessary money.[368] He was the first to hear the news. From Healy's office in the criminal court building, he rushed to a window that looked out at the jail and bellowed the news at the top of his lungs.

"A reprieve!" he shouted. "You're given until the last of August!"[369]

Hoch reportedly stood bolt upright and said, "God!" As the news spread, he heard wild cheering from the street and waved a handkerchief in his window. He shouted, "Hurrah for the Governor!" And he dabbed at his eyes.[370]

CHICAGO AMERICAN 12 O'CLOCK EDITION
SAFE-BLOWER SHOT: DYING!
HOCH'S NERVE BREAKING
POLICE HOLD CAR BANDITS

CHICAGO AMERICAN AFTERNOON EDITION
BANDITS SHOOT CONDUCTOR!
'THEY MURDER ME' CRIES HOCH IN CELL FACING GALLOWS!
Wife Poisoner Storms Violently at Execution Hour.
BANDITS ROB CAR!

CHICAGO AMERICAN AFTERNOON EDITION
SAFE-BLOWER SHOT: DYING!
HOCH'S NERVE BREAKING
POLICE HOLD CAR BANDITS

SPECIAL EXTRA SPECIAL
CHICAGO AMERICAN EXTRA
HOCH GETS HOUR MORE!
FLAMES TRAP 7; EXPLOSION; 1 HURT
FIFTY REPORTED DEAD IN WRECK
POLICE ARREST CAR BANDITS!
Fierce Storm FLOODS THE CITY!

AFTERNOON EXTRA CHICAGO AMERICAN AFTERNOON EXTRA
PLEDGE HOCH LIFE MONEY
FLAMES TRAP 7; EXPLOSION; 1 HURT
Rich Woman and Doctor in Desperate Effort to Save Him From Gallows.
Fierce Storm FLOODS THE CITY!
POLICE ARREST CAR BANDITS!

NIGHT HOME CHICAGO AMERICAN NIGHT HOME
HOCH AGAIN REPRIEVED
LIFE MONEY PLEDGED TO HOCH
FLAMES TRAP 7; EXPLOSION; 1 HURT
BULLETINS
Fierce Storm FLOODS THE CITY!

NIGHT HOME CHICAGO AMERICAN NIGHT HOME
HOCH'S LIFE IN BALANCE
LIFE MONEY PLEDGED TO HOCH
FLAMES TRAP 7; EXPLOSION; 1 HURT
BULLETINS
Fierce Storm FLOODS THE CITY

NIGHT HOME CHICAGO AMERICAN NIGHT HOME
JOHANN HOCH REPRIEVED!

CHICAGO AMERICAN NIGHT EXTRA
HOCH IN FRENZY OVER REPRIEVE
MOTHER LAYS HYPNOTISM TO YOUTH THAT WON GIRL
CONFESSES ARSON PLOT FIRE AND EXPLOSION

SPORTING EDITION SPORTING
CHICAGO AMERICAN LATEST NEWS BASEBALL
HOCH SAVED AGAIN
ARREST "SPENDER" MURDER MYSTERY
CONFESSES ARSON PLOT FIRE AND EXPLOSION
HOW HOCH WAS GIVEN REPRIEVE

CHICAGO AMERICAN EXTRA SPORTS BASEBALL
I'LL GO FREE CRIES HOCH

A montage of front pages from the various editions of the *American* that were run the day of Hoch's dramatic July 23 reprieve. *From the* Chicago American.

"It's true! It's true! It's true!" Comerford shouted, and he rushed through the corridor, down to the street, shouting out the news like Paul Revere.[371]

Jean Cowgill, the *Chronicle* feature writer, ran into a room below the "death chamber," where the officials had gathered, shouting that Hoch had been reprieved. She was nearly trampled trying to run back up the stairs to see

Hoch herself. Guards blocked her, and the *American*—the only paper to note her presence by name—said that she "created a scene."

Jailer Whitman broke down in tears. "It would have been a shame to have to hang him today just because he didn't have the money," he said. "I don't care to say anything as to his guilt or innocence."[372]

The jail maintained a schoolroom for younger inmates, and during exercise hours, Hoch had become friendly with "the boys." When Whitman told them of the reprieve, they asked to give Hoch a reception. As a surprise, Hoch was brought in on his way back to his old cell, and the boys lined up to shake his hand. As the last one passed, they broke into a chorus of "My Country, 'Tis of Thee."[373]

In a quieter moment, Hoch told a reporter that Emilie Fischer was now in New York, away from the stress. She wouldn't have gotten the news and would have assumed that he was now dead. "Perhaps it was my vanity, or whatever instinct it was," he said. "I made her promise not to read the papers....[I told her] when you come back the Reverend Mr. Schlecte will take you out to the cemetery and show you my last resting place."[374]

In reality, Fischer had taken her museum act to New York, where she would be appearing at Huber's Museum on East Fourteenth Street. She was now at third billing below Michael La Cara, a "medical marvel" whose claim to fame seems lost to history, and Sandow the Stong Man, who had been a hit at the Chicago World's Fair in 1893.

Though it was initially said that Hoch was annoyed to find out she'd be at the museum, since she hadn't promised to give him any of the money, he later said that he knew all about it. "She gets $50 a week," he said. "Why shouldn't she make what she can? I'd rather she was doing that than scrubbing office buildings or taking in boarders and getting $5 or $6 a week."[375]

It was certainly a pay cut from $250, though.

Someone may have even gone so far as to solicit funds from Minnie Warnke, perhaps even at Hoch's request. She went to the Chicago Avenue police station to rant about Hoch after the July reprieve. "He thought I was easy, but I frustrated his attempt to secure my money," she said, with evident pleasure. "He will never get one cent of my money, so he will do well not to look toward me for assistance."

Plotke told Hoch he wouldn't be able to start working on getting the case prepared right away because he would be out of town for a week. Hoch told him, "You can stay for a year if you like."[376] To a reporter, Hoch complained that on the day of the planned execution, Plotke had gone to gawk at the scaffold instead of working on a reprieve. "I don't want to get mad about the matter now that it is over," he said. "But when a man has had such a close shave as I had he can't help feeling mad at his own lawyer for 'rubbering' at the gallows."[377]

On August 1, Hoch met teenage George Plummer, who was being taken to Joliet to serve a life sentence for murder. Ruled "too small to hang," as he was only seventeen and barely four feet tall, he told Hoch he envied the quick death he'd get from the rope.

"You think I'm going to be hanged, eh?" Hoch asked. "Well, that shows you ain't smart. Johann Hoch won't be hanged. If you were smart you wouldn't have got in the fix you're in."

"How about you?" Plummer challenged.

"I'm an innocent man and everyone that thinks Johann Hoch is ever going to be hung is going to get fooled."

"Aw, you're foolin' yourself," Plummer sneered. "You ain't got a chance."

Hoch shrank away and went back to work on writing up his case, something he was now doing himself. He told Whitman he didn't want any lawyer touching his work.[378] The rush of the reprieve had worn off, and the time to get another was short.

HOCH FIRED PLOTKE AND retained Frank Comerford, the young man who'd been so excited about the reprieve, as his new lawyer. The twenty-five-year-old Comerford's reason for his interest in the case would have been obvious to insiders: he was Jean Cowgill's boyfriend.

The year before, at the age of twenty-four, Comerford had been elected to the state house of representatives. But after just a month's experience in government, he made a speech charging several members of both parties with corruption. "To say that the Illinois legislature is a great public auction where special privileges are sold to the highest corporate bidder," he said, "is to put it mildly."[379]

Members of both parties announced plans to have Comerford expelled. In the first weeks of February, stories of Hoch were often sharing space on front pages with stories of Comerford's fight at the state capitol. Representative Anton Cermak, the future mayor of Chicago, called him a double-faced liar with cigarette smoke for brains.[380] Cowgill cheered from the gallery as Comerford defended himself, but the body voted 121 to 13 to expel.

A gossip journal, *The Club Fellow*, reported that Comerford and Cowgill were engaged a month after the expulsion. Three months later came Cowgill's feature on Hoch, and a month after that, Comerford became Hoch's lawyer.

Once his services were retained, the young firebrand wrote a review of the case, including a list of arguments that Hoch should be given a new trial. Among these arguments was an insistence that Emilie Fischer was Hoch's legal wife, denying all earlier marriages. This absurd statement was mixed with more reasonable charges that the poisoning wasn't proven to everyone's satisfaction and that various "confessions" had been wrung from Hoch under duress. Other points were mainly technicalities, but might have been enough to buy Hoch some time.

With twenty-four hours to spare before the end of the second reprieve, Comerford persuaded Justice Macgruder of the state supreme court to accept the case—another dramatic rescue. Jean Cowgill was given the honor of delivering the news to Hoch.[381]

A visitor asked him if it felt good to be alive. He responded with a rambling lie about how he'd once survived a shipwreck—an old favorite—which had taught him confidence. "I will eat my Christmas dinner outside these walls," he crowed. "You will never hang Johann Hoch!"[382]

HOCH WAS ONE OF several men who spent that autumn fighting the gallows. He congratulated John Mueller, the sleepwalking killer, and Jocko Briggs every time their own reprieves came in. It's not hard to imagine the three of them comparing notes on Evelyn Campbell, who had been closely involved in all of their cases.

One conversation between the three is known: in October, someone suggested that rather than hanging, condemned men could opt to undergo dangerous experimental surgeries and be set free if they survived. Briggs rejected it. Mueller liked the idea. "You'd beat the rope, wouldn't you?" he asked. "They wouldn't get the satisfaction of killing you." He liked the idea of having a chance to live and know he'd done humanity some good either way.

"You'd have a poor chance," said Hoch. "The doctors wouldn't be very careful. They wouldn't care if you died, and they'd try all kinds of fancy things on you." He even said he'd want an assurance he *wouldn't* survive. "What's a man's life worth if he gets out and everybody points their fingers at him and calls him a murderer? Pshaw!" But he concluded he'd "rather have the doctors than the rope."[383]

There was a long history, back to the city's first hanging, of doctors being allowed to dissect bodies of condemned men after they died. Dr. Walter Haines, who'd testified against Hoch, had even been involved in experiments in the 1880s in which a team tried to resurrect a hanged man with electricity (he said they'd come pretty close).

In the end, none of the three condemned men in late 1905 resorted to any unique measures to beat the gallows. Hoch didn't even try to claim insanity. He remained confident that he'd never hang.

But on December 15, the state supreme court upheld the verdict against Hoch.

Only the governor could save him now.

23

THE PARDON BOARD

Comerford wasn't ready to give up. In January, he had Emilie Fischer swear out an affidavit stating that her sister had suffered from kidney issues for years. She now said that Marie Walcker's health had been a major factor in the misery she experienced in her marriage to Emil Walcker. She also said that Marie had confessed to her that she was suffering terribly when she married Hoch and afraid to tell her new husband about it.

Emilie also gave a second affidavit, this one seemingly more damaging. In it, she swore that the testimony she had given in the trial was given under duress. Shippy and Olson had not only forced her to live with a police officer before the trial, but they had also strongly implied that if she didn't testify against Hoch on the stand at the trial, they would charge *her* with murder, too.

It was Shippy, she said, who told her she had to go to live with a police officer "and remain in his custody day and night," during which she was to speak to no one without the officer's permission. She said she'd been told, "If I would not obey the instructions of said Inspector Shippy…I would be immediately imprisoned in the county jail." During the five weeks leading up to the trial, she'd been taken to Olson's office at all hours, often staying until after midnight, where she'd been pressured to say Hoch murdered her sister. "In addition," she noted, "they told me they had a right to arrest me as an accessory." She said she'd told them she had no way of knowing if Hoch had poisoned Marie and that if she'd seen anything to make her suspicious or seen any ill treatment, she wouldn't have married him herself.

TROOPS CLOSE HUNGARIAN PARLIAMENT

Remarkable Incidents at Budapest When Deputies Are Driven Out.

HOCH, THE SUAVE "DR. JEKYLL," AND HOCH, THE FIENDISH "MR. HYDE," THE MURDERER OF FIVE WIVES.

Remarkable Photograph by a Chicago American Staff Photographer Taken in the County Jail.

PREPARES TO SMASH HOCH'S LAST DEFENSE

State's Attorney to Send Witnesses Before the Governor.

Hoch's Nerve Giving Way.

Will Fight Life Sentence.

Still Claims Innocence.

Evidence Is Sufficient.

Marches Back to Cell.

KED BY WEST SIDE

Victim Flees for cks.

EXPOSITION OF TAFFY AND SUGAR PLUMS

Here Is Revealed With Vivid Force the Dual Personality of the Doomed Slayer of Women. First, the Pleasant, Affable "Gentleman," So Irresistible to Women, and Second, the Merciless "Bluebeard" Who Took Life Without Mercy.

FOUR MORE ALDERMEN FOR HIGH LICENSE

MAYOR DUNNE AIDS IN HUNT FOR SLUGGER

An American mock-up of Hoch photos, showing the two sides of his nature. *From the* Chicago American.

It was a damning account, but the supreme court ruled on February 8 that her statements didn't materially alter the fact that arsenic had been found in Marie's body.

The day of the ruling, Hoch was entertaining a stream of curious visitors at the jail, and by all accounts, he was in one of his better moods. The *Inter-Ocean* said that the visitors "ranged in age from 18 to 60 years and were of high and low degree."

"Good afternoon, ladies!" he greeted one group. "How are you all? I feel fine."

A timid woman in a black velvet coat asked, "Do you hypnotize women?"

"Oh, ho ho ho ho!" Hoch laughed. "Sure! Shall I hypnotize you?" He waved his hands in her face, then laughed uproariously as she shivered in fear.[384]

But in the middle of the reception, a reporter came and gave him the news of the court's latest ruling against him.

The *American* said he seemed calm at first and then said, "I believe it," over and over until he was asked if he was prepared to be executed. "No, sir!" he shouted. "Me? Execute me? Me? Hang? Never! I will get out of it some way."[385]

With no chance at a new trial, he and Comerford now had two weeks to find a miracle and secure a pardon from the governor.

A GREAT MANY PROMINENT lawyers still seemed to believe Hoch was innocent. Edmund Furthmann, who'd once offered to represent him, had died in August, but newspapers noted that Hoch was getting advice from his son, a lawyer who'd taken on some of his father's cases, and called Hoch "a friend." Others had stepped forth to help him pay for reprieves.

Comerford maintained his belief that Hoch's trial had been unfair. "Public clamor alone is responsible for Hoch's conviction," he said. "The public demanded a human sacrifice, and it didn't care one iota whether Hoch was guilty or not. Sociologists and others can say what they like, but the passions for hangings in the North is equal to the passion for lynchings in the South."[386]

Newspaper coverage of the case had surely been a factor in Hoch's conviction and sentence. Though Hoch singled out the *American*, other papers had been just as damning from the start.

But it's also quite possible that a major reason so many people believed Hoch was innocent was that the newspapers had been too squeamish to print some of the most damning evidence.

Newspapers ran large advertisements for constipation cures, laxatives, and preparations for menstrual discomfort daily, but none of the trial reporters wrote about the enemas or vaginal douches that were administered to Marie or about Emilie cleaning the "slop jar" full of her waste. People might have read doctors' claims that the arsenic in the stomach appeared to have been added after Marie was already dead, but they wouldn't have read much about the arsenic found in the rectum or colon. Newspapers certainly hadn't quoted a courtroom exchange in which Plotke asked a doctor if a bowel movement wouldn't flush all of the arsenic out of the rectum (it would not, since the "membrane of the rectum are not so very smooth") or Dr. Haines's statement that the mixing of arsenic with bloody mucus in the colon was a process that would not have happened if the arsenic had been administered after death.

Even so, the evidence *had* been circumstantial and didn't necessarily prove that Hoch had purchased the arsenic (no one ever figured out where he got it) or that he had mixed it into the enemas or medicine himself. Comerford still believed he could push the governor to commute Hoch's sentence to life imprisonment.

On February 12, Comerford and Emilie Fischer took a train to Springfield, where she was set up in the principal's office at the high school to be interviewed once again, with the school's German teacher acting as interpreter. She now denied that Hoch ever said, "The dead for the dead, the living for the living." "I was told to say these things," she testified, "by Olson."

She further reiterated that Marie had been sick for a long time, constantly bothered by kidney troubles.

This kidney trouble lay at the heart of Comerford's other secret weapon: a letter from Dr. Robert Zeit, a Northwestern University professor of pathology who had examined Marie's exhumed kidneys but hadn't testified at the trial. In a letter to the governor, touted in the press (and by Comerford) as a game changer, Zeit wrote that his own findings had been "entirely suppressed" from the testimony, and he was afraid that the state had declined to call him as a witness because it thought it might weaken its case.[387]

Many others were writing to the governor as well. One letter came from Reverend R. Keene Ryan, the *American* reporter who had covered the trial. "I never wrote you or any other governor on behalf of any man ever condemned to death in this city, although I have handled every important murder case for Mr. Hearst's papers during recent years, because I never had any doubts as to the guilt of any one of the men hanged here....But as to Hoch, I am convinced he is innocent of this crime for which he had been condemned to die, and mark my word, if we hang him every citizen in this city and state will live to regret it."[388]

Reverend Ryan also noted that everyone at the Englewood Masonic Lodge agreed with him, for what it was worth, and ranted about the laughably bad job Isadore Plotke had done as Hoch's lawyer. "Hoch is entitled to some consideration from this fact alone," he wrote.

Indeed, one move Hoch could have probably played but didn't was revealing that Plotke had been Marie Walcker's lawyer. Comerford and Ryan must not have known, or they surely would have listed it as a reason for a new trial. For reasons that can only be guessed, Hoch must have kept the information to himself.

RATHER THAN MAKE A decision on his own, Governor Deneen called witnesses to Springfield to make their case in front of board of pardons. The *American* broke out both the red ink and a couple of rarely used bubble letter fonts to announce "Bigamist Hoch's Last Chance" in its afternoon edition on February 19.

So, in what must have been a distinctly awkward train car, the witnesses for both sides assembled and traveled to Springfield to speak to the board. Olson brought along chemist Walter Haines, Inspector Shippy, a couple of other doctors, a detective or two, and Bertha Sohn. Comerford brought

CHICAGO AMERICAN'S
AVERAGE DAILY
CIRCULATION
FOR JANUARY.
351,695

CHICAGO EVENING AMERICAN

WEATHER INDICATIONS——CLOUDY.

AFTERNOON EDITION

VOL. VI., NO. 199—P. M. TUESDAY. CHICAGO, FEBRUARY 20, 1906. TUESDAY. PRICE ONE CENT.

BIGAMIST HOCH'S

LAST CHANCE

TOLEDO INSANE ASYLUM
SUPERINTENDENT TOBEY
RESIGNS UNDER FIRE!

MISER POISONED FOR $1,000,000
Unlabeled Bottles Found in Corsa Mansion in New York Point to Murder Plot.

Pardon Board at Springfield To-Day to Hea[r] New Evidence and Pleas of Lawyers.

HOPE IS WANING.

The February 19, 1906 *American* headline. *From the* Chicago American.

Dr. Zeit and Emilie Fischer. The two sisters, Bertha and Emilie, would be battling from opposite sides. If they fought on the train, it wasn't reported.

At the hearing, the two weren't called at all.[389] Most of the hearing focused on Dr. Zeit, who insisted that Marie's case of Bright's disease was bad enough that it could have killed her at any time.

In cross-examination, though, Zeit admitted that the amount of arsenic found in Marie's body would have killed her as well.[390]

Nothing was announced in time for the morning papers the next day, but the news of the pardon board's decision broke in time for the *American* to issue an extra edition in the afternoon: "Hoch to Die—MUST HANG."

24
THE FINAL DAY

Hoch woke early for his final full day, ate breakfast, and pet the two kittens that had been living in his cell. (When exactly the kittens appeared is not certain, though they were mentioned briefly in a couple of articles in different papers.)[391]

"Well, kitties," he said, "this is our last day in jail. We are going to get out of here tomorrow, and I am going to take you to Johann Hoch's place and you'll get cream three times a day for the rest of your lives, because you were a friend of the poor condemned prisoner for many terrible, lonely hours."[392]

He turned to the guards watching him and said, "Of course, you know that I am going to get out, don't you? Yes, the governor sent me a secret message saying he was going to pardon me tomorrow. Just before they come to take me to the gallows an order will come to Peters and Whitman, commanding them to give me my liberty at once. Then the doors of the jail will be thrown open and I will walk out into the sunshine free."

"Will you go back to Emilie Fischer?" a guard asked.

"Emilie Fischer? Who is she?"[393]

Though Hoch had mostly dropped the comedic persona he'd adopted in New York, just over a year before, his sense of humor was still intact. Indeed, he showed more of it on his final full day than he had in months. A young man who claimed to be a hypnotist and medical student appeared at the cell demanding to put Hoch in a trance. Hoch came up to the bars of the cell, and the young man said, "Look into my eyes."

Hoch turned his back and said, "You can look into my backside."[394]

LONG FIGHT TO SAVE HOCH MADE BEFORE PARDON BOARD

PROSECUTOR OLSON FLAYS DOOMED POISONER'S MEDICAL EXPERT

Wife Struggles at Springfield to Free Bluebeard and Murderer From Shadow of Gallows.

Continued from First Page.

PLEADS FOR PRISONER.

WIFE FAILS TO SAVE HIM.

JAILER WHITMAN PREPARES GALLOWS

CROWDS TO SEE HIM.

WORRIED?—NOT AT ALL.

JOHANN HOCH IN HIS CELL TO-DAY AND THE VISIONS THAT NEVER LEAVE HIM.

FRIENDS NOT CONFIDENT.

STRAIN OF DEATH CHAMBER.

HOCH NEVER LOST HOPE.

SPIES WATCHING CHIEF OF POLICE COLLINS?

CHICAGO WOMEN TO BE GIVEN POLICE WHISTLES

Given Permit for Whistle.

2 MYSTERIOUS FIRES UNDER INVESTIGATION

Hoch in his cell, surrounded by images of his reported victims (many of whom had long been debunked as false leads by this time). *From the* Chicago American.

But Hoch's nerves were showing. Just a week before, John Mueller, the sleepwalking murderer, had been executed after several reprieves, and Hoch was said to have been completely unnerved.

Some papers made Mueller a bigger deal than others during his trial, but his hanging hadn't been much of a story. Hoch remained a much bigger draw. As the execution approached, some papers were publishing a new edition for every tiny update. Despite Hoch's digs against the *American*, he was happy to speak with R. Keene Ryan, who was now publishing articles in the paper arguing that Hoch was innocent. When Ryan arrived at Hoch's cell the day before the hanging, he found Emilie Fischer curled up on the floor, her face wet with tears, just outside the bars. Guards hovered, making sure she wasn't slipping him any poison.

"I've met thousands of women," Hoch said, "but nowhere have I met or heard of a woman whose fidelity is equal to hers.…The evidence was all against me, but despite it all she still loves me and does everything possible to lighten the last hours of my life. I can't understand it."

"I wish I could undo the wrong I have done," Fischer said to Ryan in broken English. "I would take his place and let them hang me gladly, if they would let me. John never killed anybody."[395]

"Then why did you testify that he did?" Ryan asked her.

"I did not know what I was doing. I must have been insane. The police are to blame for all that."

Hoch spoke to Reverend Ryan about religion (all the clergy Hoch spoke to agreed that he had an excellent grasp of theology). Now and then, he casually noted the sound of the gallows being erected. Emilie remained crouched on the floor.

"According to the stories [Hoch] has told me, he has lived a charmed life," Ryan wrote. "The gallows have not been the only form of death that threatened him. In 1882 he was en route to Australia from Africa on board the steamer *La Forsa*. The steamer caught fire during the night and was burned to the water's edge. Two hundred and sixty-five lives were lost. Hoch, according to his story, was picked up by a fishing schooner next morning and carried to safety in Cape Town, the ship's only survivor."[396]

Ryan didn't have time to look up whether the sinking of *La Forsa* was even a real shipwreck. It wasn't.

The *Chronicle* painted a very different picture of Hoch's interaction with Fischer. They portrayed her begging him to understand that the police had led her to say what she did and asking, "Do you think I killed you?"

"What do I care what you said against me?" he asked. "Perhaps you'll be proud after I am dead to know that you killed an innocent man."[397]

Hoch now had a new story about Marie's death, as well: she had been an addict, and the bottles he destroyed were vials of drugs.

He was still talking to reporters when Jailer Whitman came to bring him to the death chamber.

"Excuse me," Hoch said. "I will finish the story the next time I see you."[398]

Emilie was weeping bitterly as she crept away.

Hoch refused all visitors that night, except for his spiritual advisors. To pass the time, he smoked and played cards, as most prisoners in the death chamber did.

"I will stake my life against yours on a game of seven up," he said to one guard.

"I think too much of my life to take a chance," the guard said.

"Well, I've got a whole lot of respect for my own person and I've got enough hope left to think I can win…that I will not be hung in the morning."[399]

COMPLETE RACING CHARTS IN THIS EDITION

ONE CENT CHICAGO AMERICAN AFTERNOON EDITION

HOCH SAYS: IT'S A CRIME TO HANG ME

TWO BROTHERS-IN-LAW FATALLY SHOT IN DUEL ON THE SOUTH SIDE

TATTOO MARKS SHOW MURDER VICTIM IS A MILWAUKEE MINISTER

Board of Pardons Refuses to Save Wife Murderer From Gallows To-Morrow.

PRESIDENT OF JACKSON BANK RESIGNS POST

GIRL KILLS HUSBAND TO AVENGE A SNEER

CHICAGO AMERICAN EXTRA

551,695

HOCH ACTS LIKE MADMAN

HOLDUP MAN ROBS A GIRL IN RESTAURANT

BURGLARS MENACE VICTIMS WITH DEATH!

ELGIN HAS FIRE SCARE; MICE GNAW MATCHES

GRAFT INQUIRY FOR THE STATE'S ATTORNEY

EXTRA CHICAGO AMERICAN EXTRA

HOCH PLAYS INSANITY!

BURGLARS MENACE VICTIMS WITH DEATH!

Condemned Slayer-Bigamist Begins Strange Actions in Cell in Hope to Escape Noose.

GRAFT INQUIRY FOR THE STATE'S ATTORNEY

HOLDUP MAN ROBS A GIRL IN RESTAURANT

CHICAGO AMERICAN NIGHT EXTRA

HOCH PUT IN DEATH CELL

PEACEMAKER KILLED BY HUSBAND IN FIGHT AT GRAND CROSSING

Bigamist-Murderer Gives Up All Hope of Escaping Death To-Morrow.

MIZNER, BACK IN NEW YORK, BARRED BY WIFE FROM YERKES MANSION

BURGLARS' VICTIMS ARE MENACED WITH DEATH

PROPPER DISBARRED BY STATE SUPREME COURT

CHICAGO AMERICAN EXTRA SPORTS

HOCH GIVES UP! "I DIE BRAVELY"

PEACEMAKER SHOT DEAD BY HUSBAND IN FIGHT WITH WIFE

MIZNER, BACK IN NEW YORK, BARRED BY WIFE FROM YERKES MANSION

PLUNGE ON HART TO BEAT TOMMY BURNS

PROPPER DISBARRED BY STATE SUPREME COURT

MURDERED WHILE TRYING TO SAVE WOMAN

1 CENT CHICAGO AMERICAN 8 O'CLOCK EXTRA

HOCH PLAYS HE'S INSANE

PEACEMAKER SHOT DEAD BY HUSBAND IN FIGHT WITH WIFE

Condemned Slayer Acts Strangely in Effort to Escape Death.

FLEES FOR LIFE FROM A WEST SIDE CROWD

PRAY IN CHURCH TO FIND AIDS OF IVENS

PROPPER DISBARRED BY STATE SUPREME COURT

JEW BAITERS KILL 50; PLUNDER AND BURN

Front pages from February 22, 1906, the day before Hoch's scheduled execution. *Author's collection.*

Hoch ordered a dinner of sirloin steak with onions and German-fried potatoes and then asked for a cigar. "Smoke in this world and not in the next, eh, Ernest?" he asked a guard.

The guard laughed as he gave Hoch a light.

"Life is a hot race," he said to another guard. "I've not been distanced yet. Even if I do drop out tomorrow, I'll only lose by a neck."

He looked at the silent guard. "Good joke, Wagner. Why don't you laugh?"[400]

Hoch went to bed still believing that he had an ace up his sleeve.

25

THROUGH WITH THE WORLD

The front page of the "country edition" of the *Chicago American* the day of Hoch's execution was a masterpiece of vague writing. It described the hanging in harrowing detail—the drafty corridor, the prayers, and the wild-eyed prisoner, his bravado gone as the hood was placed over his face. The terrible drop of the trapdoor.

None of this had happened yet when the paper went to press at daybreak. It wasn't scheduled to happen for several hours. The report was merely all things that surely *would* happen before the article was in the hands of a reader. The corridor was always drafty. There were always prayers. Even if something strange happened—like if the rope broke and Hoch had to be hanged twice—the article wouldn't be inaccurate. Everything it said had happened would have taken place. Later editions could add more specifics after they'd actually happened.

This sort of prewriting was not unusual, though it did sometimes lead to embarrassment, perhaps most famously a few decades later when the *Tribune* rushed out its "Dewey Defeats Truman" edition. After his reprieve in July, Hoch read in a weekly paper that he'd been executed and reportedly wrote to the editor to say, "I will be alive when you and all the dupes who read your lying sheet are dead."[401]

The prewritten account was enough for the early afternoon edition that would be sent to towns outside of the city limits, like Kankakee, Kenosha, and Racine (where savvy readers would probably be aware that it couldn't have been written, printed, and delivered in the time since the execution).

EXTRA SPECIAL EXTRA CHICAGO AMERICAN EXTRA

AND NIGHT EDITION

FRIDAY. FRIDAY.

HOCH HANGED

Johann Hoch was hanged in the north corridor of the County Jail today for the murder of his wife, Mrs. Marie Walcker-Hoch. She was the fifth wife murdered in his notorious career, according to police evidence.

The long and desperate battle of the world-notorious bigamist and murderer to defeat the ends of justice---a struggle which has no parallel in the criminal annals of the state---closed when Hoch, white-lipped and wild-eyed, was led to the gallows by Jailer Whitman and saw at last the gleaming white noose that he had seen so often in his dreams. The final moves in preparation for the hanging were brief.

During these the voice of the Rev. A. W. Schlechte, Hoch's spiritual adviser, was heard reciting prayers for the dying. Then the trap was sprung and Hoch had paid the penalty for the murder of Mrs. Walcker-Hoch, who died Jan. 11, 1905, from poison.

BODY OF HOCH IS TURNED OVER TO HIS LAST WIFE FOR BURIAL.

After the swaying body had been pronounced dead by County Physician McNamara and the jury of physicians it was lowered into a coffin and turned over to an undertaker employed by Mrs. Emilie Fischer-Hoch, the last wife of the bigamist.

The circumstances around the closing chapter in Hoch's marvelous career of lawlessness, bigamy, robbery and murder were as dramatic and fitting as even he could have wished. Not in many years--not even when the car-barn bandits were executed--was there so

The "country" edition of the *American*, which had to be printed hours early to be on the stands in outlying towns that afternoon. *From the* Chicago American.

The article would run underneath the headline, "HOCH HANGED," presented in type so large that the two words covered the entire top half of the page. The rest of the issue would be filled with stories about Hoch's final night (which was documented minute by minute), a recapping of his career, an article by Reverend Ryan and the like. The paper expected huge sales. Later editions could include details like Hoch's actual last words (though several earlier editions had a headline reading "Hoch's Last Words: 'I Am Innocent.'" Reading below would show they were *among* his "last words" in a last letter to Fischer, not what he said on the scaffold).

But the *American* should have guessed that nothing to do with Johann Hoch was ever normal. The day of his hanging would be no exception. The ordeal suffered by city editor Moe Koenigsberg as a result of forgetting this fact would become a part of Chicago newspaper legend, a story retold in taverns for decades to come. Koenigsberg himself devoted several pages in his autobiography to "the misery of my most torturous journalistic trial."

On a normal day, the *American*'s circulation was around 300,000. For the hanging, it expected 500,000, spread over the course of as many editions as possible. Before dawn, it had already run 75,000 copies of a "flash edition" with the prewritten report. These were sent off to outlying towns to await Koenigsberg's go-ahead before they were put out for sale, which he'd give the moment he knew Hoch was dead.

Every paper had its own system to alert people outside of the jail when something happened inside. For the *American*, it was a man stationed at "the doomsman's grating," a window near his position in the jail. When the "death march" from the cell to the scaffold began, he would wave a blue handkerchief at the window. That action would be seen by a man who was watching the window from the state's attorney's office, and was keeping up a phone call with the rewrite desk. A red handkerchief would mean that the trapdoor had fallen and the hanging was over.

The blue handkerchief flew at 10:05 a.m., and Koenigsberg started giving his signals to proceed.

It was several minutes later that he realized he'd never gotten a report that the red handkerchief had been waved.

Something was happening.

When he realized Hoch's execution may have been interrupted, Keonigsberg recalled, "A thunderclap out of a clear blue sky could not have been more stunning to me.…Either Johann Hoch must be promptly hanged, or I must slink in shame out of the fourth estate."

HOCH HAD AWAKENED IN the death chamber at 6:30 a.m. For his last meal, he ordered ham and eggs with the ham bone left in.

"Boy, this certainly is a fine breakfast," he said, as he read about himself in the papers. As he finished his eggs, he looked to a guard and said, "How would you like to change places with me?"

"Well, I don't know," the guard replied.

"But I insist on an answer," said Hoch.

"I think you have got something up your sleeve. I don't believe you have the slightest intention of going to the gallows. Yes, John, you certainly have something up your sleeve."

Hoch winked, put a finger over his eye, and said "Just watch Johann Hoch."[402]

There was, in fact, a new attempt to save him underway. Frank Comerford had enlisted Edward Maher, an older attorney, to help get another delay. Though none of the papers mentioned it at the time, Maher had represented H.H. Holmes in several early swindling cases, perhaps most notably in cases with the architect and steel company who'd built the "Castle" building in

1887 (whom Holmes had declined to pay). He had parted ways with Holmes before his cases got darker, but now, he had joined the ranks of lawyers who believed that Johann Hoch deserved another chance.

At 9:00 a.m., Comerford, his partner J.J. Neiger, and Maher appeared at the federal building and obtained a writ of habeus corpus. Hoch, Comerford explained, had been arrested for bigamy in New York, only to be tried for murder in Chicago. This, they claimed, was not due process. Writ in hand, Comerford hastened to the jail, pushing through the throng that had gathered outside the door, shouting, "Send Whitman here! I've got a stay!"[403]

Deputy Sheriff Peters and Jailer Whitman looked at the paperwork. "This petition acts virtually as a stay," Comerford said. "If the petition is denied, we shall appeal the case, and you will have no right to hang Hoch until this appeal is decided."[404]

The two officials weren't sure this was correct, but agreed to delay the execution long enough to give Comerford a chance to get the petition approved or denied by a judge. The three attorneys jumped into a cab to return to the federal building.[405]

Hoch, being told that there was a delay, turned to his companions with a smile and said, "Well, boys, I'm hungry. Let's have dinner."[406]

The *American*'s article hadn't included the exact time of the execution—it hadn't even said "morning" but "today." As long as the hanging took place, the article in that "flash extra" could still be accurate in all particulars when it hit the stands.

Fortunately, the noon edition in the city hadn't announced the hanging; the headline read "Hoch Dressed for Gallows," which was true.

Reporters trailed Comerford and Maher right into the office of the famous Judge Kenesaw Mountain Landis.

Judge Landis, whose stern countenance made one critic liken him to "Whistler's mother in slacks," was a staunch moralist who chomped cigars and swore freely. He would later find fame as the first commissioner of Major League Baseball, the man who banned the "Black Sox" of 1919 from the game for life. Leo Durocher would say that the team owners who gave Landis his commission "got him right out of Dickens." Not quite forty but already topped by his trademark white hair, Landis was new to the bench in 1906, but crucially for Hoch's lawyers, he was already known to be unpredictable and enough of a character that the reporters looking for a story could usually get one just by hanging around his courtroom. This suited Landis, a shameless publicity hound, just fine.

After listening to Comerford and Maher's points, Landis asked if they were trying to say there was an error in the court's decision because the date read "June" instead of "February."

"No, we do not raise that point," said Comerford, explaining that they believed only Hoch had been held without due process of law in the first place.

The unpredictable Judge Kenesaw Mountain Landis, who would find his greatest fame as the commissioner of Major League Baseball. *Library of Congress.*

Landis seemed skeptical and said they should have gotten a writ of error instead. They rushed off to get another appeal bond and brought it back to Landis, who told them it would have to be signed by the prisoner.[407]

Comerford raced to the jail to get the signature, and Landis retired to his chambers.

News of the development spread. Back at the *American*, Koenigsberg was in a panic, calling his contacts at the courthouse. None would make any bets as to what Landis would do.

Maher paced outside the chamber door until Landis emerged again, now dressed in his street clothes.

"Won't you wait for us a few minutes longer?" asked Maher. "We have only a little time. A man's life is at stake, and the papers will be here in a few minutes."

"I am going out to lunch now," said Landis. "I will be in court at two o'clock."

"My god, Judge! Don't leave the building. Please don't do it. Give this man the right of an appeal. At two o'clock, this man will be dead."[408]

"You make it awful hard for me," said Landis, possibly just referring to the fact that Maher was blocking him from getting to the elevator, "but as I told you, I cannot grant an appeal. My oath of office demands that I do what I consider right....I do not think I would be complying with my oath if I delayed the hanging."

"Judge, if I didn't think this poor man had a fair chance, I wouldn't make this appeal to you," Maher begged. "What errors in delays his attorneys have made shouldn't cost him his life when there is still a way open. Grant me this right of appeal, and don't leave the building until you have done so."[409]

"I don't think I can," said Landis.

Maher held a watch in front of Landis's face. "Look here. See how the minutes are going? At two o'clock this man will be dead. For God's sake, don't go."

For a moment, Landis stared, astonished at this outburst. "The pallor of the jurist," noted the *Inter-Ocean*, "was visibly contrasted with the flushed face of the attorney."

Unpredictable as the judge was, it was easy to imagine him saying, "By God, you're right!" and ordering the execution stopped, if only for the amount of publicity it would bring him. But it wasn't to be.

"I have expressed my views on the subject of an appeal," Landis said. "And I will not grant one. There is no use of my remaining."[410]

And he stepped into the elevator, leaving Maher behind, just moments before Comerford and Neiger arrived with Hoch's signature on the bond.

A messenger boy arrived with a telegram for Landis, and someone told the boy that the judge would be at the Great Northern Hotel for lunch. The three dashed off to find him there, but he wasn't present. They tried the Union League Club and the Chicago Club, but again, the judge was nowhere to be seen.

And by now, they knew, it was too late.[411]

It was warm for February. The *Inter-Ocean* estimated that five thousand people crowded the sidewalks, some of them laughing and singing songs.

At 1:28 p.m., having been informed by Landis that he should proceed with the hanging, Jailer Whitman came into the cell.

RESPECT MOTHER, HOCH'S WARNING

REV. R. KEENE RYAN IN REMARKABLE EXCLUSIVE INTERVIEW WITH POISONER

NERVE OF PRISONER ADMIRED

This remarkable interview with Johann Hoch, the bigamist and condemned to be hanged to-day for poisoning one of his wives, was secured to-day by the Rev. R. Keene Ryan for the Chicago American. Throughout the trying hours just previous to the time set for his execution Hoch was cheerful, optimistic, even joking. His optimism and his regard for his mother and a mother's advice and love were marked.

BY THE REV. R. KEENE RYAN.

"RESPECT your mother."

There never was a greater optimist than Johann Hoch.

LOOKS AT HIM IN GREAT AMAZEMENT

"IT'S THE CARPENTERS BUILDING THE GALLOWS," he replied, as calmly and unconcernedly as if he had said "It's the prisoners at play."

READY TO GO TO DEATH, CHAMBER AND CHEERFUL

HOW JOHANN HOCH MARCHED TO THE GALLOWS

Remarkable Picture of the Actual Procession to the Gallows by American's Photographers and Art Staff.

Heading the procession to the gallows was Chief Deputy Sheriff Peters. Jailer Whitman at his left and Night Jailer O'Neill at his right guarded Hoch. The Rev. A. W. Schlechte, Hoch's spiritual adviser, followed.

JOKES ON EVE OF HIS EXECUTION

SPECULATES ON THE LIFE IN THE NEXT WORLD

"EASIER TO TELL OTHER PEOPLE WHAT TO DO"

"DON'T HANG ANY MORE MEN IN THIS CITY"

EVERY MAN, WOMAN AND CHILD IN THIS STATE IS RESPONSIBLE FOR JOHANN HOCH'S DEATH.

"MOST FOOLISH USE OF ME IS TO HANG ME"

The *American*'s mock-up of what the procession to the scaffold would have looked like. *From the* Chicago American.

"I am ready," said Hoch. He shook hands with a few people, and said, "Goodbye, boys."

"Do you wish to say anything from the gallows?" he was asked.

"Johann Hoch is through with the world. I haven't a word to say."

So, the death march began, and the hanging of Johann Hoch proceeded just as the *American* had written the night before, except Reverend Birkelund was behind Hoch, replacing Haertel, a discrepancy no one noticed.

Prayers were read, and Hoch, looking at the assembled group of doctors, reporters and officials, said, "Oh lord, our father, forgive them all. They know not what they do. They hang an innocent man. I am innocent. Goodbye."

It was, in essence, just what the *American* had advertised as his last words.

Moments later, the trapdoor fell, and Johann Hoch's neck was broken.[412]

26

THE AFTERMATH

At 2:15 p.m., in a characteristically unpredictable after-lunch move, Judge Landis granted Comerford and Maher's appeal. But Hoch had been pronounced dead half an hour before.

This would make for controversy the next day, as Comerford announced that he would have Whitman and every other official involved in the hanging indicted for murder.

"I think it would have been a purely arbitrary exercise of judicial power to have interfered in the matter," said Landis, who was, of course, known to pursue such arbitrary exercises now and then. "The lawyers came in here with their petition and stormed and said that 99 percent of the people were opposed to the hanging of this man, that I would be mobbed when I left the court, and asked me to decide judicially a point on public sentiment. When they filed the appeal bond I approved it, just as I would approve any other bond which I believed to be a good bond. But what effect it will have I do not know."[413]

If Landis had not gone to lunch, Hoch might not have been hanged. Olson, in fact, thought Comerford and Maher had come awfully close to freeing him. "The habeus corpus petition was a trick of the lawyers to save Hoch's neck," he said. "They sought to deceive the sheriff into delaying the execution. Had they succeeded today, they would have sprung another habeus corpus action and demanded Hoch's liberty. Their chances of success would have been bright."[414]

CHICAGO AMERICAN'S CIRCULATION 551,695

CHICAGO AMERICAN

12 O'CLOCK EDITION

HOCH DRESSED FOR THE GALLOWS

With all hope of a respite abandoned, Johann Hoch early today dressed for the gallows and sat calmly awaiting the arrival of the Sheriff for the march to his death.

STORY OF HOCH'S LAST NIGHT IN DEATH CELL

WOMAN TRAIN WRECKER HYPNOTIZES IN COURT

Tiffin, O., Teacher Has Mania to See Suffering, Say Police.

PRIMARY DAY TO-MORROW; BOTH PARTIES

COUNTY BOARD UNDER GRAFT INQUIRY THREAT

COMPLETE RACING CHARTS IN THIS EDITION

ONE CENT

CHICAGO AMERICAN

AFTERNOON EDITION

"I'LL NOT HANG" SAYS JOHANN HOCH

MIZNER, BACK IN NEW YORK, BARRED BY WIFE FROM YERKES MANSION

Attorney for Man Condemned to Death Makes New Move to Stay Execution.

PEACEMAKER SHOT DEAD BY HUSBAND IN FIGHT WITH

50 JEWS KILLED BY MOBS

PROPPER DISBARRED STATE SUPREME

"I WRECKED TRAINS," SAYS

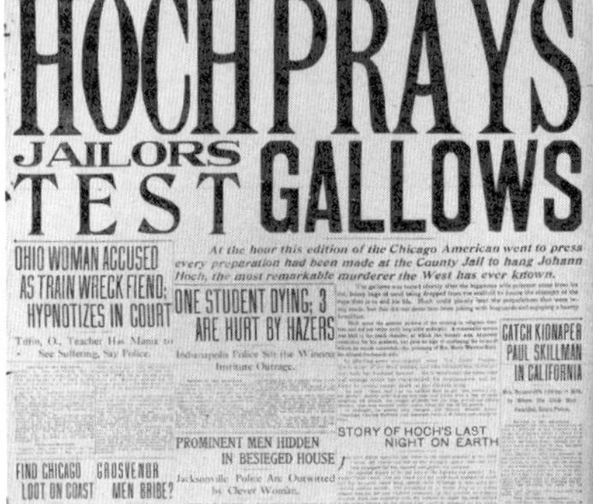
CHICAGO AMERICAN'S CIRCULATION 551,695

CHICAGO AMERICAN

AFTERNOON EDITION

HOCH PRAYS

JAILORS TEST GALLOWS

At the hour this edition of the Chicago American went to press every preparation had been made at the County Jail to hang Johann Hoch, the most remarkable murderer the West has ever known.

OHIO WOMAN ACCUSED AS TRAIN WRECK FIEND; HYPNOTIZES IN COURT

Tiffin, O., Teacher Has Mania to See Suffering, Say Police.

ONE STUDENT DYING; 3 ARE HURT BY HAZERS

Indianapolis Police Set the Witness... Institute Outrage.

CATCH KIDNAPER PAUL SKILLMAN IN CALIFORNIA

STORY OF HOCH'S LAST NIGHT ON EARTH

PROMINENT MEN HIDDEN IN BESIEGED HOUSE

Jacksonville Police Are Outwitted by Clever Woman.

FIND CHICAGO LOOT ON COAST

GROSVENOR MEN BRIBE?

CHICAGO AMERICAN'S CIRCULATION 551,695

CHICAGO AMERICAN

AFTERNOON EXTRA

ASK U. S. COURT TO STOP HANGING

HOCH'S LAST WORDS "I AM INNOCENT"

"My Dear Wife: This is the last letter I can write you. The end draws near. I know and you know I am innocent of this crime. So, good-by, Emilie. This is my last letter.

"Yours in death as in life,

"JOHANN."

Hoch's Attorney Appeals to the Federal Judiciary for a Stay at Last Hour.

18 CONTESTS IN 15 WARDS

POLICEMAN RESCUES 5 CHILDREN FROM FIRE

NORTHERN PAC. IS UP 2 POINTS

WHEAT AT NEW

STORY OF HOCH'S LAST NIGHT IN DEATH CELL

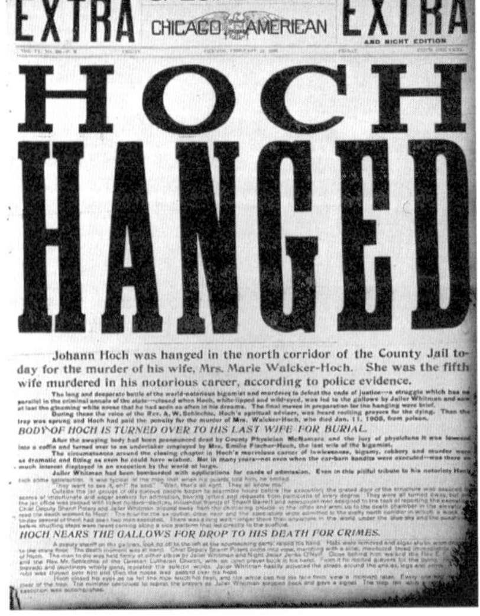
EXTRA

SPECIAL EXTRA

CHICAGO AMERICAN

EXTRA

AND NIGHT EDITION

HOCH HANGED

Johann Hoch was hanged in the north corridor of the County Jail today for the murder of his wife, Mrs. Marie Walcker-Hoch. She was the fifth wife murdered in his notorious career, according to police evidence.

BODY OF HOCH IS TURNED OVER TO HIS LAST WIFE FOR BURIAL.

HOCH NEARS THE GALLOWS FOR DROP TO HIS DEATH FOR CRIMES.

FIRST INSIDE STORY OF MIZNER'S MARRIAGE PLOT

Night and Home Edition

CHICAGO AMERICAN

HOCH HANGED!

After Fight for Delay at the Eleventh Hour, Bigamist-Murderer Dies on Gallows.

STORY OF HOCH'S LAST NIGHT IN DEATH CELL

POLICEMAN AT FIRE RESCUES FIVE CHILDREN

WOMAN HORSEWHIPS MAN RIVAL IN FLOWER BUSINESS

Mrs. Schuler Attacks E. F. Ams, Who, She Says, Defamed Her.

Front pages of various editions from February 23, 1906. *Author's collection.*

In any case, nothing came of the plot to have Whitman or anyone else arrested. Papers and lawyers speculated about the issue for a couple of days, and then the story faded away.

Hoch had likely died the moment the trapdoor fell due to a broken neck. It was noted that his heartbeat did not cease for thirteen minutes, but this was normal for hangings. "He died easily and painlessly," said physician McNamara. "He was practically dead, I believe, the instant the rope tightened at the end of the drop."[415]

In 1936, McNamara reminisced about the day with a *Tribune* reporter. With glib sexism, he spoke of the way Emilie Fischer had come to the jail to collect Hoch's remains and personal effects. "She had forgiven him," he said, "and now she was preparing to weep over the worthless articles he had left behind. You can learn about women from her."[416]

Fischer spent the morning of the execution at her new apartment on Wells Street. She was distressed when given the news of Hoch's death but denied plans to kill herself.

"Poor Hoch," she said. "They have hanged an innocent man. He did not kill my sister. He is the most maligned man on the earth. He had but one wife, and I was that woman. This talk of his having had fifty wives is all a lie. He was neither a bigamist nor a murderer. My sister died of kidney trouble. The arsenic they found in her body was deposited there by the embalming fluid. Hoch did not steal my money, I gave it to him. I loved him all along, and I will love his memory as that of a good and kind man until I die."[417]

In Philadelphia, Caroline Streicher believed she knew through some sort of telepathy the moment Hoch's death came.

"Some time after one o'clock," she said, "something like a great blur came before my eye and everything in the room seemed dark to me for a while. I believe that he was dying at that moment. I called to my daughter to play the piano and as she did so I arose and waltzed about the room for sheer joy. How I ever escaped death at the hands of that villain is a marvel to me. Ever since he left the house—some of his things are still here—I have felt a terrible dread that I was not yet out of his clutches....Thank God, it is all over."[418]

Hoch, for the record, was still alive for some time after her vision.

Prisoners cast lots for some of Hoch's personal effects that Emilie didn't take. One prisoner got Hoch's carpet, another his alarm clock.[419]

The *Daily News* noted that Nicholas Wagner, a guard, was given a book by Hoch. It's unclear whether this was the manuscript of the book Hoch had claimed he was writing. It's possible, though on his last day, Hoch had joked that all of his talk of writing a book before had just been a ruse to make money.

"I never wrote a book, and never intended to," he told the *Inter-Ocean*. "I had some bids, but they were all for confessions. I was told that if I would admit that I killed a number of women I would be paid well for it. A man who would make such a suggestion deserves to be swindled!" He hinted that he'd taken several advances from the publishers but had never given them the manuscripts he promised. "Oh, John is foxy, all right!"[420]

But it was also reported that he was scribbling furiously during his last couple of days. Several guards reportedly got to see a bit of his work, and one guard, perhaps Wagner, was able to get a few pages to the *American*, which worked them into its later articles on hanging day. They consisted of Hoch rambling about how it felt to be in the death cell, digesting his sirloin steak and waiting to die, apparently on the June night when he got a reprieve. It may have been real. But if there was more of a manuscript, it was soon lost.

Emilie Fischer and an undertaker arrived at the jail in a carriage that afternoon to claim the body. Most of the larger cemeteries in Chicago had already refused to bury Hoch, so Emilie and a minister went first to St. Lucas Cemetery on the west side, where they were turned away. Then they went to Forest Home in the west suburbs, where they were first accepted and then, after the cemetery officials reconsidered, turned away. Running out of daylight, they hastened to Dunning, the pauper's cemetery on the northwest side, where groundskeepers agreed to "shelter" the coffin, at least for the time being.[421]

The next morning, with Emilie too sick to continue searching, Hoch's body was buried at Dunning. A few days later, Elmwood Cemetery agreed to take the body, and the remains were moved to the quiet burial ground in the west suburbs. No marker was ever put in place.

EPILOGUE

Several mysteries remain about Hoch. In prison, he occasionally alluded to one particular secret he would take to his grave.

Jack Lait, an *American* reporter, would claim, through some hazy memories forty-three years later, that the "richest feature" of the case was that Hoch had been doing all of his swindling to support one woman he truly loved, one whose name somehow stayed out of the story. Lait said she had been a waitress when Hoch met her, but by 1905, she was living off his money, never asking where he got it. When Lait suggested that she send flowers to the funeral, she told him, "Listen, reporter, every nickel I got out of that walrus I earned. I'm kicking back nothing."[422]

Some retellings of the case repeated rumors that in order to ingratiate himself to women, Hoch would claim to have a chemical preparation that helped with menopausal discomfort. His comments to Marie Walcker about seeing lots of women undressed may support this.

A further theory was that he, as a chemist, was only doing experiments with arsenic and never meant to kill anyone.

Another theory held that he truly believed himself to be innocent, as he never *technically* administered the poison himself; it had been always someone else who actually administered the medicine or enemas.

And some who met him really did seem to believe that his five dead wives had all died of natural causes.

Why exactly Johann Hoch chose to poison Marie Walcker is a question the state never adequately answered. Marie, who had a small amount of savings, was the sort of woman he normally merely deserted; the others who died tended to have far more property. That he'd spent several weeks poisoning her on the off chance that he could woo and propose to Emilie in front of her sister's corpse seems like ridiculously risky scheme, and the $750 he stole from Emilie was hardly a fortune, either. He'd made far more with a lot less trouble before. Even if it had been the plan, extracting money from a wife *and* her sister before leaving town was a trick he'd pulled off before without resorting to murder.

If Hoch really did have a dark secret that explained everything, he kept his promise and took it to his grave.

NANA SPRINGER, ALIAS EVELYN Campbell, married Matty White of the *Tribune* in the spring of 1907.[423] Throughout 1908, she wrote articles for another Hearst paper, the *Chicago Examiner*, most of which were about women in sports fandom.

She drifted away from journalism after her children were born, but in 1915, Moe Koenigsberg needed a writer to pen a fictional domestic serial and thought of her. Under the name Adele Garrison, she began writing "Revelations of a Wife," in nine-hundred-word daily installments, and kept the story going for over forty years.

Living in Long Island in the 1920s, she would often drive through Manhattan, the scene of her and Anna Hendricks's triumph over Hoch. Once, while driving with a reporter who was doing a profile on her, she took a hard curve around Central Park Avenue that got her car onto one wheel, and said, "Driving gives me some of the thrills I used to get when I was Evelyn Campbell!"[424]

In 1948, after writing nearly ten million words of her serial, she said, "My granddaughter claims I'm the godmother of all the soap operas, but I'd give my right leg to go out on a good news story again."[425]

She died in 1956 at the age of eighty-three. In articles about her early life, people remembered two things: her efforts had saved the life of the innocent Jocko Briggs, and her work ended the career of the guilty Johann Hoch.

A month after Hoch's death, Frank Comerford and Jean Cowgill went to St. Joseph, Michigan, to get married. Jean had just written a story on the town and its reputation for being a place for quickie weddings.

Weeks later, Mayor Dunne named Frank special attorney to the police department. When Dunne was ousted the next year, it was alleged that Comerford and Chief Collins had used the police force to manipulate the election in Dunne's favor, among other abuses of power; both Collins and Comerford ended up on trial for corruption in 1908. Comerford was acquitted and later became a judge.

Jean Cowgill spent much of the 1910s running the Illinois Woman's Press Association, a position she sometimes used to pushed for women's suffrage.[426]

The couple were divorced in 1921, and Frank died of a heart attack in 1929. Jean moved to California and eventually became editor of a small paper, *The Los Altos News*, a job she held until her retirement in 1944. She died four years later.[427]

Reverend R. Keene Ryan would go on to spend years serving on the board of pardons and paroles. He made a lot of enemies, some of whom had him arrested on a trumped-up charge of being a German spy during World War I. The charge was dismissed quickly but became a news story anyway. "Judge [Kenesaw Mountain] Landis has a grudge against me," he explained, "and would like to get a chance to send me to jail, [so he] notified papers of my arrest."[428]

A few years later, Landis and Ryan buried whatever hatchet was between them long enough to share speaking duties at baseball star Cap Anson's funeral.

In 1917, Coroner Peter Hoffman ruled that a man who died after molten metal was poured on him at a factory had actually died of tuberculosis,[429] sparing the factory and insurance companies from any payouts to the family. It was, by then, one item in an endless list of reasons to think Hoffman was not exactly honest.

In 1907, he had deliberately sabotaged an autopsy whose results might have exonerated accused poisoner Herman Billik. Shippy, now newly appointed as chief of police, had already coerced a young boy into giving testimony implicating Billik. The boy later recanted, saying the chief had threatened to hang *him* if he didn't say he'd seen Billik mixing poisons, even though he really hadn't. Shippy and Hoffman got the conviction they wanted, but Billik was almost certainly innocent. Fortunately, he was pardoned before he could be hanged, though he still went down in history as a serial killer.

Less than a year after Shippy became chief, an eighteen-year-old Russian immigrant named Lazarus Averbuch came to his Lincoln Park home, possibly believing he needed a letter of good character from the chief of police to get a job out of town, as had been the custom in the old country. Shippy, noting that Averbuch looked Jewish and assuming him to be an anarchist, shot him to death. Whether Averbuch was looking for trouble was never determined. At the coroner's inquest, Shippy claimed he had acted in self-defense against an assassin, and only one person was allowed to ask any questions: Hoffman. Shippy was cleared of wrongdoing, but he never spent another day in uniform. He was showing signs of dementia, possibly due to syphilis, and when "rest cures" taken after the inquest didn't help, he resigned. He became violent and paranoid around his family and died two months after being sent to an asylum in 1913.

Hoffman became sheriff in the 1920s but was caught giving special treatment to gangsters, presumably in exchange for bribes, and ended up doing time in his own jail. Reporter Ben Hecht's newsroom play *The Front Page* contains a bumbling, corrupt sheriff, "Peter Hartman," who is eager to hang an innocent man in order to look tough before an election. Clearly based on Hoffman, the character is described in the stage directions as "an overwrought little fellow, an incompetent fuss budget."

While few would doubt that Hoch killed Marie Walcker, the mere fact that Hoffman and Shippy were involved leaves several details open to skepticism. If one or both of them had arranged for several grains of arsenic to be added to the stomach of Walcker's corpse to ensure a conviction (unaware that it could already be found in her rectum), it wouldn't have been the only time the Chicago authorities pulled dirty tricks to frame a guilty man.

THOUGH ARSENIC'S INCLUSION IN embalming fluid fell out of favor, it continued to be a popular murder weapon in Chicago.

In 1913, the *New York Sun* ran an article in which chemist Walter Haines said he was sure that "hundreds [of] murderers walk the streets of Chicago today whose crimes are never suspected....I should say that for every poison murder detected at least three are never discovered. The ratio may be much higher." Coroner Hoffman said it was probably at least eight to one. Olson, now Chief Justice Olson of the municipal court, said it was more like twelve.[430]

MARIA JULIA DOESS, THE Cincinnati wife, died of stomach trouble in 1906, only months after Hoch was hanged.[431] Minnie Lembke Westphal of New York died in 1936; Amanda Dickhuth of New York died in 1912; and Caroline Streicher of Philadelphia died in 1940.

Maximilliana Sperl, an early Chicago Hoch wife, met an eighty-three-year-old man through a matrimonial advertisement in 1903, married him after two weeks, and ended up divorcing him in 1905.

Martha Hertzfeld, the Chicago Hoch wife who moved to Pasadena, married the much older Henry Hammelgarn in September 1906. When Henry died in 1912, she was left with a small fortune. She died in Los Angeles in 1945, the same year Bertha Sohn died in Chicago.

Nannie Von Klencke of Baltimore died in 1941. Her son, John J. Klencke, who had been nineteen years old and possibly still living with her when Hoch moved in, came to be known as a "man of many aliases" himself. The alias that stuck was "Baltimore Johnny." After living a long life of crime, he was wanted for stealing cases of whiskey when he was shot down by gangsters in 1926.

IT WAS REPORTED IN 1907 that Emilie Fischer and Minnie Warnke had gone on the vaudeville circuit together shortly after the hanging, but little data remains to back it up.[432]

In 1915, Minnie Warnke, alias Ernestine Domke, Emma Rankin, Minnie Renken, and several others, was found sick and nearly starving in a small apartment a mile or so northwest of the jail. She was taken to the hospital, where she soon died. The *Tribune* noted, "In the room was found a veritable storehouse of furs, silk gowns, and expensive articles of women's wear.... Neighbors were unable to explain the presence of the expensive garments." She was buried in Montrose Cemetery.[433]

The paper recalled that Mrs. Warnke and Hoch had "a fine time" calling each other 'bluebeard' when she was brought to confront him, but it also told a few stories about her that were actually about Elizabeth Goerk.

Goerk was gone by then; her 1913 obituary didn't mention Hoch, but it did mention the loss of her stepdaughter in the Iroquois Theatre fire as one of the "sad incidents" that had weighed on her mind and damaged her mental health. She spent the last year of her life in an asylum in Elgin, Illinois, where, per the obituary, "Death came as a welcome messenger and delivered her from all evil." She was buried in Iowa.[434]

CATHERINE KUMERLE WAS TRACKED down by the *New York Daily News* in 1926. She was destitute, living in a sparse room on East 115th Street, but she was still willing to reminisce about Hoch peeling potatoes.

She'd never gotten the money the police had promised her, and the publicity had been so bad for her business that she changed her name. After a nervous breakdown, she found work as a nurse but got a chicken bone caught in her throat that couldn't be removed, even surgically. It caused her to cough so much that people thought she was sick, which cost her job after job. "What life holds for her next she does not know," wrote the *News*, "but there is still no lack of courage in the woman."[435]

ANNA HENDRICKS MAY HAVE changed her name as well. A city directory from 1906 lists her as the widow of Henry Hendricks and living on Fortieth Court (now South Komensky Street), where she'd lived since Henry was alive. But

The gravestone Hoch purchased for Henry Hendricks, covered in cicadas in 2024. *Photo by the author.*

she was gone from the directory the next year, and from there, her trail appears to grow cold. The gravestone Hoch bought for her first husband still stands at Forest Home Cemetery, one of the burial grounds that refused to bury Hoch himself.

EMILIE FISCHER MADE THE papers one more time. In late 1907, she married a man named Frank Stein, who knew her only as "Emilie Fischer" and had no idea of her connection to Hoch.

Only a few months after the wedding, she called the police and said Frank had thrown a beer glass at her. In response, he told the police a few stories about Emilie.

"She showed me the rope with which Hoch was hanged, Judge," Frank told the court, "and said that strangling me with that would be too good for me. She boasted that she had caused her first husband to be hanged and that she would serve me the same or worse. She crushed my new hat with a loaf of bread and beat me over the head and face with a roast duck."[436] He had already packed his trunk to move out.

Emilie is not known to have tried marriage again, though she lived for nearly three more decades.

All of this certainly says *something* about Fischer's behavior during the whole Hoch saga, but it's hard to say just *what*.

A granddaughter of Emilie who recalled meeting her once spoke of her in hushed tones and was certainly under the impression that there was something scandalous in her background. She believed that, being in Chicago, "Grandma Fischer" had run a boardinghouse that was a safehouse for the mob—or something like that. "Pure imagination," her own grandson said.[437]

Most of her children eventually joined her in Chicago, and family photos from the 1920s show both her and Bertha, reconciled enough to at least pose in the same picture. Upon her death in 1934, she was buried at St. Lucas Cemetery, a cemetery that had turned Hoch down.

The approximate location of Hoch's unmarked grave in River Forst, Illinois. *Photo by author.*

EPILOGUE

JOHANN HOCH'S UNMARKED BURIAL spot at Elmwood Cemetery was a term grave, leased for only thirty years. When the term was up, no one offered to renew it, and the section of the cemetery where Hoch had been buried was redeveloped. It's impossible to locate his precise burial place today, but it's near the Elmwood Chapel. Strangely, it's likely some place between a marker for a family named Schmidt, his real last name, and the grave of a woman named Elizabeth Weber, his mother's maiden name.

Just a coincidence.

APPENDIX

KNOWN WIVES

Many papers published lists of Hoch's various wives, though no two lists looked remotely the same. The *Daily News* got a list of twelve from Olson (all correct but with the dates imperfect). The *Chronicle* and *Post* each put the number of wives at fourteen. The *Journal* put the number at thirty-five but included in its list names such as Julie Laclerque and Wilhelmina Scheldemantel, characters who had almost certainly been invented for the *American*'s "How I Married Fifty Women" fairy tale the previous July.

These are the ones I find most likely to be real, including their dates of marriage, their city, the name Hoch used, and the reason for separating from Hoch. A few of them have never been mentioned as Hoch wives before.

1890
Christine Ramb, Germany, as Jacob Schmitt (deserted).

April 1895
Caroline Hoch, Wheeling, as Jacob Huff (died after three months).

August 1895
Julia Steinbrecher, Chicago, as Johann Hoch (died after four months).

January 1896
Minnie Warnke, Chicago, as Johann Hoch (mutual desertion).

April 1896
Martha Hertzfeld, Chicago, as Johann Adolph Hoch (deserted).

August 1896
Barbara Bossert, San Francisco, as Jacob Schmitt (deserted).

October 1896
Clara Bartels, Cincinnati, as Jacob Schmitt (died after a few months).

March 1897
Maria Julia Doess, Cincinnati, as Jacob Schmitt (deserted).

May 1897
Barbara Chuston, Philadelphia, as Frederick W. Doessing (deserted).

July 1897
Margaret "Maggie" Koelle, Brooklyn, as Frederick William Doessa (deserted).

August 1897
Maximilliana Sperl, Chicago, married in Milwaukee as Fred W. Doesing (deserted).

December 1897
Amanda Baertz Dickhuth, New York, as Fred Doering (deserted).

January 1898
Minnie Lembke, Jersey City, as Fred Doesing (deserted).

March 1898
Elizabeth Schmitz, Milwaukee, as Frederick W. Doesing (deserted).

November 1901
Mary Elizabeth Goerk, Chicago, as Jacob Schmitt (deserted).

April 1902
Mary Becher, St. Louis, as John Schultz (died after eleven months).

January 1904
Anna Mary Hendricks, Chicago, as John Jacob Schmitt (deserted).

July 1904
Nannie Von Klencke, Baltimore, as John Schultz (deserted).

October 1904
Caroline Streicher, Philadelphia, as John Schmidt (deserted).

December 1904
Marie Schippnick Walcker, Chicago, as Johann Hoch (died after five weeks).

January 1905
Emilie Schippnick Fischer, Chicago, as Johann Hoch (deserted).

NOTES

Introduction

1. Frances Maule, "Hoch Jokes About His 'Dear Wives' on Way to Chicago," *New York American*, February 9, 1905.
2. "Hoch Happy, Near Chicago," *Chicago Evening Journal*, February 9, 1905.
3. "Hoch Indicted," *New York Telegram*, February 1, 1905.
4. "Hoch Seen at Close Range," *Chicago Journal*, February 10, 1905.
5. "Hoch Happy," *Chicago Journal*.

Chapter 1

6. "The Deadly Ice Water," *Wheeling Daily Intelligencer*, July 8, 1898.
7. "A Murder Mystery," *Wheeling Daily Intelligencer*, September 20, 1898.
8. "Want the Body Exhumed," *Wheeling Register*, November 3, 1898.
9. "Murder Mystery," *Wheeling Daily Intelligencer*.
10. "Down to Death," *Wheeling Daily Intelligencer*, January 31, 1895.
11. "It Deceived Nobody," *Wheeling Register*, July 4, 1895.
12. "Small Talk," *Wheeling Sunday Register*, February 2, 1895.
13. "Hoch Poisoned a Wife as He Kissed Her," *New York American*, February 9, 1905.
14. "Dr. Ford's Statement," *Wheeling Register*, November 4, 1898.
15. "Hoch Poisoned a Wife," *New York American*.
16. *Hannoverscher Kurier*, March 2, 1905.
17. *Aus Mustis Blauerede*, June 25, 1905.
18. *Hannoverscher Kurier*, March 2, 1905.
19. "Kontours," *Allemeigne Zeitung*, January 13, 1905.

Chapter 2

20. "Trace Hoch to New York," *Chicago Tribune*, January 28, 1905.
21. "Death of One Wife Gives Hoch $4000," *Chicago Journal*, January 25, 1905.
22. "Death of One Wife," *Chicago Journal*.
23. "Trace a Bluebeard," *Chicago Chronicle*, January 23, 1905.
24. "Death of One Wife," *Chicago Journal*.
25. Graceland Interment Book, death certificate.
26. "Sure Hock Slew Her," *Chicago Post*, January 24, 1905.
27. "Death of One Wife," *Chicago Journal*.
28. "Hoch's Opinion," *New York Dispatch*, September 1, 1905.
29. "Find Hoch's Drugs," *Chicago Chronicle*, January 26, 1905.
30. "More Spouses of Hoch Come Forward," *San Francisco Examiner*, February 4, 1905.
31. "Spouses of Hoch Come Forward," *San Francisco Examiner*.
32. "Deluded by Doesing," *Appleton Post*, October 13, 1898.
33. "She Lost Jacob and Her Money," *San Francisco Call*, August 27, 1896.
34. "She Lost Jacob," *San Francisco Call*.
35. "Loses Her Cash and Her Husband," *San Francisco Chronicle*, August 27, 1896.
36. "She Lost Jacob," *San Francisco Call*.
37. "Bluebeard Hoch Had Carried Dagger in Umbrella," *San Francisco Chronicle*, February 17, 1905.
38. "Hoch Had Carried Dagger," *San Francisco Chronicle*.
39. "She Lost Jacob," *San Francisco Call*.
40. "Hoch Had Carried Dagger," *San Francisco Chronicle*.
41. "Bigamy," *Cincinnati Enquirer*, February 2, 1905.
42. "Did Hoch Poison?" *Butler County Democrat*, February 16, 1905.
43. *Cincinnati Enquirer*, February 2, 1905.
44. "She Did Not Like Schmitt," *Cincinnati Post*, February 11, 1905.
45. "Hoch's Career in Cincinnati," *Cincinnati Post*, February 1, 1905.
46. "Twice Married in Cincinnati…," *Cincinnati Enquirer*, February 1, 1905.
47. "Bigamy," *Cincinnati Enquirer*, February 1, 1905.
48. "Did Not Like Schmitt," *Cincinnati Post*, February 11, 1905.
49. "A Glass of Wine," *Cincinnati Enquirer*, February 2, 1905.
50. "Glass of Wine," *Cincinnati Enquirer*.
51. "Would Try to Bring Hoch…," *Cincinnati Post*, February 9, 1905.
52. "Plenty of Liquor," *Cincinnati Enquirer*, February 2, 1905.
53. "Says Hoch Cried for First Wife at the Funeral of Mrs. Bartel," *Cincinnati Post*, February 11, 1905.
54. "Plenty of Liquor," *Cincinnati Enquirer*.
55. "Glass of Wine," *Cincinnati Enquirer*.

56. "Hoch Cried for First Wife," *Cincinnati Post.*
57. "Hoch's Hypnotic Eye," *Cincinnati Post*, February 11, 1905.
58. "Would Try to Bring Hoch," *Cincinnati Post*, February 9, 1905.
59. "Would Try to Bring Hoch," *Cincinnati Enquirer*, February 2, 1905.
60. "Johann Hoch, Chicago's Alleged Bluebeard," *Butler County Democrat*, February 9, 1905.
61. "Chicago's Alleged Bluebeard," *Butler County Democrat.*
62. "Chicago's Alleged Bluebeard," *Butler County Democrat.*
63. "Much Married Doesing," *Wisconsin Leader*, October 9, 1898.
64. "Advertised for Wives," *Baltimore Sun*, October 10, 1898.
65. "Powder May Be Poison," *New York Tribune*, February 7, 1905.
66. "List of Wives Grows," *Chicago Daily News*, February 6, 1905.
67. "2 Wives Claim Hoch Here," *New York Evening World*, February 6, 1905.
68. "Powder May Be Poison," *New York Tribune*; figures are also in "Five More Wives Found," *New York American*, February 7, 1905.
69. "Much Married Doesing," *Wisconsin Leader.*
70. *Milwaukee Journal*, April 11, 1895.
71. "Her Wedding," *Milwaukee Journal*, April 5, 1898.
72. "Bluebeard," *Milwaukee Journal* , February 11, 1905.
73. "Wird Irrsinnig," *Abendblatt*, April 14, 1898.
74. "Death of One Woman Gives Hoch $4000," *Chicago Evening Journal*, January 25, 1905.
75. "Doessing Is a Trickster," *Chicago Daily News*, October 8, 1898.
76. "Deluded," *Appleton Post*, October 13, 1898.
77. "Spouses of Hoch Come Forward," *San Francisco Examiner.*
78. "Dollars vs. Crime," *Milwaukee Journal*, August 2, 1899.
79. "Murder Mystery," *Wheeling Daily Intelligencer.*
80. "Ford's Statement," *Wheeling Register.*
81. "Will Be Exhumed," *Wheeling Intelligencer*, November 5, 1898.
82. "Mrs. Huff's Body Exhumed," *Wheeling Register*, November 14, 1898.
83. "He Will Escape," *Wheeling Intelligencer*, November 15, 1898.
84. "Bluebeard Hoch a Murderer Says Pastor," *New York American*, February 9, 1905.
85. "He Will Escape," *Wheeling Intelligencer.*
86. "More Wives of Hoch," *Chicago Daily News*, January 30, 1905.
87. "One of Wives," *Des Moines Register*, February 4, 1905.
88. "More Wives," *Chicago Daily News.*
89. "Hock Taken by Gotham Police," *Chicago Daily Inter-Ocean*, January 31, 1905.
90. "Hock Taken," *Chicago Daily Inter-Ocean.*
91. "More Wives," *Chicago Daily News.*
92. "Hock Taken," *Chicago Daily Inter-Ocean.*

93. "Autocratic Manners Made Johann Hoch, the Believed Wife Poisoner, a Marked Man in the St. Louis Shop Where He Told," *St. Louis Post-Dispatch*, January 27, 1905.
94. "Autocratic Manners," *St. Louis Post-Dispatch.*
95. "Autocratic Manners," *St. Louis Post-Dispatch.*
96. "Autocratic Manners," *St. Louis Post-Dispatch.*
97. "Wives and Poison in Hock History," *Chicago Tribune*, January 24, 1905.
98. "Police Call Hock World's Greatest Poisoner," *Chicago Evening American*, January 25, 1905.
99. "Autocratic Manners," *St. Louis Post-Dispatch.*
100. "Autocratic Manners," *St. Louis Post-Dispatch.*
101. "Autocratic Manners," *St. Louis Post-Dispatch.*
102. "Autocratic Manners," *St. Louis Post-Dispatch.*
103. "World's Greatest Poisoner," *Chicago Evening American.*
104. "Autocratic Manners," *St. Louis Post-Dispatch.*
105. "Autocratic Manners," *St. Louis Post-Dispatch*, January 25, 1905.
106. "No Use to Disinter Mrs. Schulz's Body," *St. Louis Post-Dispatch*, April 7, 1905.
107. Evelyn Campbell, "Police of Two Continents Seek Poisoner Johann Hoch," *Chicago Evening American*, January 28, 1905.
108. Mary Hendricks (though probably written by Evelyn Campbell), "Kumerle Wife," *Chicago American*, February 3, 1905.
109. Hendricks (Campbell), "Kumerle Wife."
110. Campbell, "Police of Two Continents."
111. Evelyn Campbell, "Kumerle Wife Tells of Hock's Perfidy," *Chicago Evening American*, February 2, 1905.
112. Hendricks (Campbell), "Kumerle Wife."
113. *Chicago Evening American*, February 2, 1905.
114. Anna lived on Fortieth Court (now South Komensky Avenue), according to one newspaper article and the city directories. More articles had her living on Union Avenue, but she told Evelyn she'd been employed there.
115. *Chicago Evening American*, February 2, 1905.
116. Campbell, "Wife Tells of Hock."
117. Campbell, "Police of Two Continents."
118. Campbell, "Police of Two Continents."
119. "Five Hoch Wives Die," *Chicago Journal*, January 24, 1905.
120. Campbell, "Police of Two Continents."
121. "Hock Buries One, Weds 2d, Proposes to 3d in a Week," *Chicago Evening American*, January 31, 1905.
122. "Hock Buries One," *Chicago Evening American.*
123. "Married at Towson," *Baltimore Sun*, February 3, 1905.
124. "Hoch in This City," *Baltimore Sun*, February 2, 1905.

125. "Widower Weds Widow at Towson," *Baltimore Sun*, July 4, 1904.
126. "Hoch's Wives Dead and Living Number 21," *New York American*, February 2, 1905.
127. "Hoch in This City," *Baltimore Sun*.
128. "Woman Tells…," *New York Journal*, January 31, 1905.
129. "May Have Escaped Death by Poison," *Philadelphia Inquirer*, January 30, 1905.
130. Trial transcript.
131. "May Have Escaped Death," *Philadelphia Inquirer*.
132. "May Have Escaped Death," *Philadelphia Inquirer*.
133. "May Have Escaped Death," *Philadelphia Inquirer*.
134. "May Have Escaped Death," *Philadelphia Inquirer*.
135. "May Have Escaped Death," *Philadelphia Inquirer*.
136. "May Have Escaped Death," *Philadelphia Inquirer*.

Chapter 3

137. *Walcker v. Walcker*.
138. "Woos Wife and Dies," *Chicago Chronicle*, January 21, 1905.
139. "Hoch's Trip a Triumph," *Chicago Daily News*, February 9, 1905.

Chapter 4

140. This line is usually said to have come from a World War I–era article by Arthur Peglar, but it might have been invented by Ben Hecht (who was talking about Chicago papers, not Hearst papers) years later. The origins of these things are hazy; much of what we *think* we know comes from mid-century reporter memoirs that are less reliable than any of their actual reporting.
141. George Murray, *Madhouse on Madison Street* (Follett, 1965), n.p.
142. "Vendettas of the Evening Papers," *Chicago Chronicle*, July 30, 1905.
143. "Vendettas," *Chicago Chronicle*.
144. Moses Koenigsberg, *King News* (F.A. Stokes, 1941), n.p.
145. "Exhume Bride's Body," *Chicago American Night Extra*, January 20, 1905.

Chapter 5

146. "Tells of Poison Plan," *Chicago Daily News*, January 25, 1905.
147. "Was Holmes Janitor?" *Chicago Sun*, January 23, 1905.
148. "Hock Accused by Dying Wife as Her Poisoner," *Chicago American* (noon edition), January 23, 1905.

Chapter 6

149. *True Republican* (Sycamore, IL), March 29, 1905.
150. "Adele Garrison at 75 Keeps Serial Running," *Editor and Publisher*, March 27, 1948.
151. "Hock Clews Weighed Ounce by Ounce," *Chicago American*, January 26, 1905.
152. "Hock Arch Fiend and Poisoner," *Chicago Evening American*, January 26, 1905.
153. "Mrs. Domke Ill in Jail," *Chicago Chronicle*, April 6, 1897.
154. "Son Accuses Mrs. Domke," *Chicago Chronicle*, April 7, 1897.

Chapter 7

155. "Secrets of Hock's Power Revealed," *Chicago American*, January 26, 1905.
156. "Hock Case Lays Bare Crimes of Marriage Agencies," *Chicago American*, January 30, 1905.
157. Campbell, "Police of Two Continents."
158. Campbell, "Police of Two Continents."
159. Evelyn Campbell, "Hoch Was an Accomplice of Holmes, Says Woman," *Chicago American*, January 31, 1905.
160. "Hoch's Hypnotic Eye," *Cincinnati Post*, February 11, 1905.
161. "Hock Clews Weighed," *Chicago American.*

Chapter 8

162. "Hock Read Murder News," *New York Journal*, January 31, 1905.
163. "Brands Hoch Slayer," *Chicago Daily News*, January 31, 1905.
164. "How Wooing Won Hock's Arrest," *Chicago American*, February 6, 1905 (uncredited but presumed to have been written by Evelyn Campbell).
165. "Tells How 'Bluebird' Hoch Wooed and Nearly Won Her," *New York Herald*, February 7, 1905.
166. "Woman Tells Story of Betraying Hock," *Chicago American* (noon edition), January 31, 1905.
167. "Woman Tells," *New York Journal.*
168. "This Bluebeard Used Much Money in Wooing," *New York Daily News*, January 31, 1905.
169. "How 'Bluebird' Hoch Wooed," *New York Herald.*
170. "Woman Tells Story," *Chicago American.*
171. "Bluebeard's Captor Destitute," *New York Daily News*, August 1, 1926.
172. "Woman Tells Story," *Chicago American.*
173. "Johann Hoch, the Chicago Bluebeard, Caught," *New York American*, January 31, 1905.
174. "Woman Tells," *New York Journal.*

175. "Hoch Had Hypnotic Power," *New York Journal*, February 7, 1905.
176. "Captor Destitute," *New York Daily News*.
177. "Bluebeard, Caught," *New York American*.
178. Trial transcripts.
179. "Hoch, Chicago Bluebeard, a Prisoner Here," *New York World*, January 31, 1905.
180. "Hoch Taken by Gotham Police," *Chicago Daily Inter-Ocean*, January 31, 1905.
181. "Woman Tells Story," *Chicago Evening American*.

Chapter 9

182. "Woman Tells," *New York Journal*.
183. "Arsenic Found in the Body of Bluebeard's 25th Wife," *New York American*, February 1, 1905.
184. "Arsenic Found," *New York American*.
185. "Poison Found in Stomach of Mrs. Hoch," *Chicago Evening Journal*, January 31, 1905.
186. "Hoch Wives Number 31," *New York American*, February 2, 1905.
187. "Hoch Ridicules Charge, Admits Two Wives Only," *New York American*, February 2, 1905.
188. "Poison Found," *Chicago Evening Journal*.
189. "Poison Found," *Chicago Evening Journal*.

Chapter 10

190. "Votes to Indict Hoch," *Chicago Daily News*, February 1, 1905.
191. Campbell, "Police of Two Continents."
192. "Woman Picks Out Hoch," *Chicago Journal*, February 2, 1905.

Chapter 11

193. Campbell, "Wife Tells of Hock."
194. *Chicago Evening American*, the rest of this section can be found in "Dramatic Scene," *New York Journal*, February 3, 1905.
195. "Hoch Laughs at His Accusers," *Chicago American*, February 4, 1905.
196. This exchange was widely reported but is absent from the surviving editions of the *Evening American*.
197. "Hoch Now Admits Three Marriages," *New York Herald*, February 5, 1906.
198. "Hoch Laughs," *Chicago American*.
199. "Hoch Laughs," *Chicago American*.
200. "Hoch Wife Poisoned," *Chicago Daily News*, February 4, 1905.

201. "Hoch Laughs," *Chicago Evening American.*
202. "Hoch Tells Story," *Chicago Evening American,* February 4, 1905.
203. "Hoch Will Be Indicted," *Chicago Journal,* February 4, 1905.
204. "Fourteen Wives to Meet Hoch at the Depot," *New York American* Feb 5, 1905
205. Evelyn Campbell, "They've Got Me for Bigamy I Suppose," *Chicago American,* February 4, 1905.
206. "Bluebeard Talk of All New York," *Chicago Tribune,* February 5, 1905.

Chapter 12

207. Evelyn Campbell, "Arsenic in Hock's Room," *Chicago American,* February 6, 1905.
208. Evelyn Campbell, "Hock Won Widows and Their Money by Hypnotism!" *Chicago American,* February 7, 1905; "Poison Pen Found," *New York Journal,* February 6, 1905.
209. "How 'Bluebird' Hoch Wooed," *New York Herald.*
210. Campbell, "Arsenic."
211. "Hoch a Murderer," *New York American.*
212. "He Poisoned Me," *New York Journal,* February 7, 1905.
213. "Married For Money, Not Love," *New York Journal,* February 14, 1905.

Chapter 13

214. "Hoch in Chicago This Afternoon," *Chicago Tribune,* February 9, 1905.
215. "Bluebeard Triumphal," *New York Sun,* February 9, 1905.
216. "Bluebeard Hoch Off for Chicago," *New York Mail,* February 8, 1905.
217. "Hoch Starts to Chicago Cheerfully Talkative," *New York Press,* February 9, 1905.
218. "Bluebeard Triumphal," *New York Sun.*
219. "Part in Cupid Plot Owned by Hoch Wife," *Chicago Daily Inter-Ocean,* February 8, 1905.
220. "Hoch Off for Chicago," *New York Mail.*
221. "Hoch Starts to Chicago," *New York Press.*
222. Evelyn Campbell, "Hoch Defies All," *Chicago Evening American,* February 9, 1905.
223. Campbell, "Hoch Defies."
224. Campbell, "Hoch Defies."
225. Campbell, "Hoch Defies."
226. "Hoch Is Happy," *Chicago Journal,* February 9, 1905.
227. "Wives See Hoch," *Chicago Chronicle,* February 10, 1905.
228. Maule, "Hoch Jokes."
229. Maule, "Hoch Jokes."
230. Maule, "Hoch Jokes."

231. Maule, "Hoch Jokes."
232. Evelyn Campbell, "Hoch Defies All," *Chicago American*, February 9, 1905. A slightly different version of this article can be found in the *New York Journal.*
233. "Wives See Hoch," *Chicago Chronicle.*
234. "Hoch Admits Carelessness," *New York World*, February 9, 1905.
235. "Hoch Confesses as He Is Taken West," *New York World*, February 9, 1905.
236. Campbell, "Hoch Defies All."
237. "Hoch Confesses," *New York World*, February 9, 1905.
238. "Hoch Confesses," *New York World.*
239. Campbell, "Hoch Defies All."
240. "Johann A. Hoch in Fort Wayne," *Fort Wayne Daily News*, February 9, 1905.
241. "Hoch Happy," *Chicago Journal.*
242. Evelyn Campbell, "Betrayed? No! I Gave Myself Up," *Chicago American*, February 10, 1905.
243. "Hoch in Fort Wayne," *Fort Wayne Daily News.*

Chapter 14

244. "Hoch Owns Up to Nine Wives," *Chicago Tribune*, February 10, 1905.
245. "Hoch Owns Up," *Chicago Tribune.*
246. "Wives See Hoch," *Chicago Chronicle*, February 10, 1905.
247. "Wives See Hoch," *Chicago Chronicle.*
248. "Hoch Owns Up," *Chicago Tribune.*
249. "Hoch Owns Up," *Chicago Tribune.*
250. "Hoch Owns Up," *Chicago Tribune.*
251. "Hoch Owns Up," *Chicago Tribune.*
252. "Hoch Owns Up," *Chicago Tribune.*
253. "Hoch Owns Up," *Chicago Tribune.*
254. "Hoch's Trip," *Chicago Daily News.*
255. "Wives See Hoch," *Chicago Chronicle* (the *Chicago Chronicle* mixed up Minnie Rankin and Elizabeth Goerk).
256. "Wives See Hoch," *Chicago Chronicle.*
257. "Wives See Hoch," *Chicago Chronicle.*
258. "Wives See Hoch," *Chicago Chronicle.*
259. "Wives See Hoch," *Chicago Chronicle.*
260. "Wives See Hoch," *Chicago Chronicle.*
261. *Chicago Evening American*, February 10, 1905.
262. *Chicago Evening American*, February 10, 1905.
263. "Wives See Hoch," *Chicago Chronicle.*

264. Trial transcript.
265. "Hoch Returns to Chicago Cheerfully," *Chicago Daily Inter-Ocean*, February 10, 1905.

Chapter 15

266. Plotke, passport application, 1912.
267. "Hoch Seen," *Chicago Journal*.
268. "Smiles at His Accusers," *Chicago Sun*, February 10, 1905.
269. "Hoch Forgets Wives," *Chicago Chronicle*, February 11, 1905.
270. "Hoch Jests No Longer," *Chicago Journal*, February 10, 1905.
271. "Hoch Accused by Wife," *Chicago Daily News*, February 10, 1905.
272. "Hoch, Before Jury, Shows He Is Tired," *Chicago Record Herald*, February 11, 1905.
273. "Forgets Wives," *Chicago Chronicle*.
274. "Forgets Wives," *Chicago Chronicle*.
275. "Forgets Wives," *Chicago Chronicle*.
276. *Streator Times*, February 10, 1905; and others.
277. "Forgets Wives," *Chicago Chronicle*.
278. "Hoch Unmoved by Charges," *Chicago Daily Inter-Ocean*, February 11, 1905.
279. "Forgets Wives," *Chicago Chronicle*.
280. "Forgets Wives," *Chicago Chronicle*.
281. "Bluebeard Was Married Five Times in Milwaukee," *Milwaukee Journal*, February 11, 1905.
282. "Hoch at Inquest of Wife's Body," *Chicago Tribune*, February 11, 1905.

Chapter 16

283. "Coddle Hoch," *Chicago American*, February 11, 1905.
284. "Murder Confession from Hoch Awaited," *Chicago Daily Inter-Ocean*, February 12, 1905.
285. "Hoch Has Severe Disappointment," *Chicago Evening American*, February 12, 1905.
286. "Hoch Given Outing," *Chicago Chronicle*, February 12, 1905.
287. "Hoch Given Outing," *Chicago Chronicle*.
288. "Police Make Hoch Happy," *Chicago Tribune*, February 12, 1905.
289. "Hoch Demands Proof," *Chicago Daily News*, February 11, 1905.
290. "Severe Disappointment," *Chicago Evening American*.
291. "Hoch Holmes Aid," *Chicago Journal*, February 12, 1905.
292. "Bigamist Hoch Gets an Offer," *Chicago Tribune*, February 14, 1905.
293. "Grand Jury Will Consider Hoch," *Chicago Journal*, February 11, 1905.
294. "Grand Jury," *Chicago Journal*.

295. "Hoch Sees Face of Dead Wife," *Chicago Journal*, February 15, 1905.
296. "Murder Confession," *Chicago Daily Inter-Ocean*.

Chapter 17

297. "Hoch Greets Friend," *Chicago Chronicle*, February 14, 1905.
298. "Hoch Holmes Aid," *Chicago Journal*.
299. Evelyn Campbell, "Picks Hoch as Poisoner, Holmes Aid, at Castle," *Chicago American*, February 12, 1905.
300. "Hoch Holmes Ally," *Chicago American*, February 13, 1905.
301. "Hoch Greets Friend," *Chicago Chronicle*.
302. "Bigamist Hoch," *Chicago Tribune*.
303. "Hoch Greets Friend," *Chicago Chronicle*.
304. "Bigamist Hoch," *Chicago Tribune*.
305. "Says Hoch Isn't Jake," *Chicago Daily News*, February 14, 1905.
306. "Hoch Not with Holmes," *Chicago Journal*, February 14, 1905.
307. "Hoch Greets Friend," *Chicago Chronicle*.
308. "Mysterious Hoch Not Holmes Friend," *Philadelphia Inquirer*, January 27, 1905.

Chapter 18

309. "Hoch Facing an Ordeal," *Chicago Chronicle*, February 15, 1905.
310. "Hoch Jeered," *Chicago Evening American*, February 14, 1905.
311. "Hoch as a Rich Man," *Chicago Evening Post*, February 15, 1905.
312. "Prisoner Hoch Shown Face of Dead," *Chicago Journal*, February 15, 1905.
313. "Did Hoch Poison Wife?" *Chicago Daily Inter-Ocean*, February 16, 1905.
314. "Jury Learns Hoch's Past," *Chicago Tribune*, February 16, 1905.
315. "Tells of Hoch's Life," *Chicago Daily News*, February 15, 1905.
316. "Hoch's Life," *Chicago Daily News*.
317. "Hoch Denies Confession," *Chicago Daily News*, February 21, 1905.
318. "Mrs. Fischer Accused as Hoch's Aid," *Chicago Journal*, February 17, 1905.
319. "Aims to Clear Hoch," *Chicago Record-Herald*, February 9, 1905.
320. "Fischer Accused," *Chicago Journal*.
321. "Hoch Wives in Paris," *Chicago Journal*, February 16, 1905.
322. "Hoch Had Wives in Europe Too," *New York American*. February 17, 1905. The quote is confirmed in the *Daily News* but not included in full.
323. Evelyn Campbell, "Prefers a Broom to Notoriety," *Chicago American*, February 18, 1905.
324. "Hoch Is Held to Jury," *Chicago Daily News*, February 23, 1905.
325. "To Release Hoch," *Chicago Post*, February 24, 1905.

Chapter 19

326. Herbert Harley, "Hon Harry Olson," *The Broad Ax* (Chicago), December 22, 1923.
327. Harry Olson, "Crime and Heredity," *Journal of the American Judicature Society* (August 1923): n.p.
328. "Chief Justice Olson Kills Color Line," *Chicago Defender*, August 29, 1914.
329. Olson, "Crime and Heredity."
330. Harley, "Olson."
331. "Edmund Furthmann Will Be Leading Counsel," *Chicago Journal*, February 21, 1905.
332. "Hoch Jury Filled, State Thwarts Plot," *Chicago Daily Inter-Ocean*, May 2, 1905.
333. "Friend Will Try Hoch," *Chicago Daily Inter-Ocean*, April 25, 1905.
334. "Hoch in New Defense," *Chicago Daily News*, April 21, 1905.
335. "Bad Luck," *Milwaukee Journal*, April 21, 1905.
336. "Jury Sends Hoch to the Gallows," *Chicago Tribune*, May 21, 1905.
337. "Jury Has Hoch Case," *Chicago Evening Post*, May 19, 1905.
338. "The Hoch Verdict," *Chicago Tribune*, May 2, 1905.
339. "Gallows for Hoch," *Chicago Chronicle*, May 20, 1905.
340. "Gallows for Hoch," *Chicago Chronicle*.
341. "Conviction of Hoch," *Butler County Democrat*, May 25, 1905.
342. "Jury Dooms Hoch to Gallows for Wife's Murder," *Chicago Daily Inter-Ocean*, May 20, 1905.
343. "Hoch to the Gallows," *Chicago Tribune*.
344. "Hoch Gives Clew to His Secret," *Chicago Tribune*, May 21, 1905.
345. "Hoch Weeps and Insists 'It's a Shame,'" *Chicago Journal*, May 20, 1905.

Chapter 20

346. *Custer Weekly Chronicle*, April 1, 1893.
347. Jean Comerford, "IWPA Notes," *The Scoop*, January 11, 1913.
348. Geraldine Todd, "Jean Cowgill Comerford," *Daily Palo Alto Times*, August 22, 1946.
349. *The Club Fellow*, March 22, 1905.

Chapter 21

350. *Chicago Daily News*, June 20, 1905.
351. "Hoch Happy Beyond Words," *Daily* (Springfield) *Illinois State Register*, June 24, 1905.
352. R. Keene Ryan, letter to Charles Deneed, February 18, 1906, Hoch Clemency File.
353. "Newspaper Woman in the City," *Daily* (Springfield) *Illinois State Register*, June 23, 1905.
354. "Murderers Exchange Congratulations," *Allen County Republican*, June 27, 1905.

355. Augusta Pio, "Views on Many Topics," *Chicago Daily News*, August 17, 1905.
356. "Hoch to Die, Deneen Says," *Chicago Journal*, July 27, 1905.

Chapter 22

357. "Prize Fight to Help Hoch," *Chicago Daily News*, July 17, 1905.
358. "Death Watch Over Hoch! Hanging Near," *Chicago American*, July 17, 1906.
359. "Johann Hoch to Die Today; His Final Appeal Fails," *Chicago Daily Inter-Ocean*, July 28, 1905.
360. "Hoch to Die Today," *Chicago Daily Inter-Ocean*.
361. "Hoch Dies Today for Lack of $600," *Chicago Tribune*, July 28, 1905.
362. "How Hoch Spent Night Facing Doom," *Chicago Evening American*, July 28, 1905.
363. "Hoch Dies Today," *Chicago Tribune*.
364. "Hoch Saved by Money," *Chicago Chronicle*, July 29, 1905.
365. "Saved by Money," *Chicago Chronicle*.
366. "Wife Slayer Snatched from Gallows at Last Hour," *Chicago American*, July 28, 1905.
367. "Hoch Is Saved from Gallows by Narrow Margin," *Chicago Daily Inter-Ocean*, July 29, 1905.
368. "Hoch Is Saved," *Chicago Daily Inter-Ocean*.
369. "Saved by Money," *Chicago Chronicle*.
370. "Slayer Snatched from Gallows," *Chicago American*.
371. "Slayer Snatched from Gallows," *Chicago American*.
372. "Saved by Money," *Chicago Chronicle*.
373. "Saved by Money," *Chicago Chronicle*.
374. "Slayer Snatched from Gallows," *Chicago American*.
375. "Hoch Takes Control of Affairs," *Chicago Journal*, August 1, 1905.
376. "Wife Refuses to Aid Bigamist Hoch," *Chicago Daily Inter-Ocean*, July 30, 1905.
377. "Hoch Sore at His Attorney," *Fargo Forum*, August 1, 1905.
378. "Boy Sentenced to Life," *Chicago American*, August 2, 1905.
379. "Move to Expel Graft Accuser," *Chicago Tribune*, February 1, 1904.
380. "Comerford Is Fired by the Illinois House," *Davenport Daily Times*, February 9, 1905.
381. "Hoch's Life Saved; Issue Order for Supersede as Writ," *Daily* (Springfield, IL) *Illinois State Register*, August 24, 1905.
382. "Hoch Saved from Gallows," *Chicago Evening American*, August 24, 1905.
383. "Saleys in New Role," *Chicago Daily News*, October 26, 1905.

Chapter 23

384. "Hoch Again Under Noose," *Chicago Daily Inter-Ocean*, February 9, 1906.
385. "Hoch Loses Fight for Life," *Chicago American*, February 8, 1905.
386. "Hoch Confesses Suicide Plot," *Chicago American*, February 9, 1906.

387. Zeit, letter to Deneed, Hoch Executive Clemency File, Illinois State Archives.
388. Ryan, letter to Deneed.
389. "Hoch to Hang Friday, Says All Right," *Chicago Journal*, February 21, 1906.
390. "Hoch's Final Plea Made," *Chicago Tribune*, February 21, 1906.

Chapter 24

391. "Hoch Plays Insanity," *Chicago American* (extra), February 21, 1906.
392. "Plays Insanity," *Chicago American* (extra).
393. "Plays Insanity," *Chicago American* (extra).
394. "Halt Sich Tapfer," *Chicago Abendpost*, February 22, 1906.
395. R. Keene Ryan, "Gives Eleven Reasons Why He Should Live," *Chicago American*, February 22, 1905.
396. R. Keene Ryan, "Nerve of Prisoner Admired," *Chicago American*, February 23, 1905.
397. "Hoch Faces Gallows," *Chicago Chronicle*, February 23, 1906.
398. Ryan, "Nerve of Prisoner."
399. "Hoch Faces Gallows," *Chicago Chronicle*.
400. "Hoch Hanged, Cries 'Innocent' to Very Last," *Chicago American*, February 23, 1906.

Chapter 25

401. "Hoch Reads of Own Hanging," *Galena Gazette*, August 5, 1905.
402. "Hoch Hanged," *Chicago Journal*.
403. "Johann Hoch Is Hanged, Says He Is Innocent," *Chicago Daily News*, February 23, 1906.
404. "Hoch Pays Penalty, Court Refuses Aid," *Chicago Post*, February 23, 1906.
405. "Hoch Pays Penalty," *Chicago Post*.
406. "Hoch Is Hanged," *Chicago Daily News*.
407. "Hoch, Denying His Guilt to the End, Is Hanged," *Chicago Inter-Ocean*, February 23, 1906.
408. "Denying His Guilt," *Chicago Inter-Ocean*.
409. "Denying His Guilt," *Chicago Inter-Ocean*.
410. "Denying His Guilt," *Chicago Inter-Ocean*.
411. "Denying His Guilt," *Chicago Inter-Ocean*.
412. "Denying His Guilt," *Chicago Inter-Ocean*.

Chapter 26

413. "Was Habeus Corpus a Plot to Free Hoch?" *Chicago Daily News*, February 24, 1906.
414. "Habeus Corpus a Plot?" *Chicago Daily News*.
415. "Preacher Takes Hoch's Body," *Chicago American* (8:00 extra), February 23, 1906.
416. Francis McNamara and Charles Collins, "Drama in the Death House," *Chicago Tribune*, December 13, 1938.

417. "Hoch Hanged," *Chicago Journal.*
418. "Ex-Wife Waltzed as the Drop Fell Under Johann Hoch," *Philadelphia Inquirer*, February 24, 1906.
419. "Hoch's Body Buried in the Potter's Field," *Chicago American*, February 24, 1906.
420. "Hoch to Go to Gallows," *Chicago Inter-Ocean*, February 23, 1906.
421. "Preacher Takes Hoch's Body," *Chicago American* (8:00 extra).

Epilogue

422. Jack Lait, "Broadway and Elsewhere," *Camden Courier*, July 2, 1949.
423. "White-Springer," *The Joliet News*, April 18, 1907.
424. "Reveals Author of 'Revelations of a Wife,'" *Spokane Daily Chronicle*, March 14, 1922.
425. "Garrison at 75," *Editor and Publisher.*
426. Jean Comerford, "IWPA Notes," *The Scoop*, October 24, 1912.
427. "Death Takes Mrs. Comerford, Writer and Early Day Actress," *Palo Alto Times*, July 16, 1948.
428. "Rev Keene Ryan," *Democrat and Leader* (Russelville, KY), May 11, 1917.
429. "Fee System in Coroner Office," *Chicago Tribune*, December 9, 1918.
430. "Murder Detection Science," *New York Sun*, February 16, 1913.
431. "One Hoch Wife Dead," *Eagle River Review*, August 24, 1906.
432. "License Echoes Hoch Trial," *Joliet Herald*, June 16, 1907.
433. "Widow of Hoch Found Starving; Has Costly Gowns," *Chicago Tribune*, December 1, 1915.
434. "Mary Maass-Goerk," *Greene Recorder*, October 22, 1913.
435. "Captor Destitute," *New York Daily News.*
436. "Wed Hoch's Widow and Is Sorry," *Chicago Daily News*, June 3, 1908.
437. Personal interview with author, 2023.

ABOUT THE AUTHOR

Jen B.

Adam Selzer is a tour guide, historian, and podcaster. He is the author of more than twenty books, including *Graveyards of Trinity Church and St. Paul's: A History and Guide*, *Graceland Cemetery*, *HH Holmes: The True History of the White City Devil*, and several novels. Find him online and sign up for a tour, virtual or in-person, at adamchicago.com.